Ed Sheeran.

Published by
Wise Publications
14-15 Berners Street, London W1T 3LJ, UK.

Exclusive Distributors:
Music Sales Limited
Distribution Centre, Newmarket Road,
Bury St Edmunds, Suffolk IP33 3YB, UK.

Music Sales Pty Limited
20 Resolution Drive, Caringbah,
NSW 2229, Australia.

Order No. AM1004300
ISBN: 978-1-78038-402-3
This book © Copyright 2011 Wise Publications,
a division of Music Sales Limited.

Edited by Jenni Norey.
Music arranged by Vasco Hexel.
Music processed by Paul Ewers Music Design.

Printed in the EU.

Ed Sheeran

WISE PUBLICATIONS
part of The Music Sales Group

London / New York / Paris / Sydney / Copenhagen / Berlin / Madrid / Hong Kong / Tokyo

The A Team

Words & Music by Ed Sheeran

Drunk

Words & Music by Ed Sheeran & Jake Gosling

1. I wan-na be drunk when I wake up, on the right side of the wrong
2. I wan-na hold your heart in both hands, not watch it fiz-zle at the bot-tom of a Coke can.

bed and nev-er an ex-cuse I made up. Tell you the truth I did what
And I got no plans for the week-end, so should we speak then? Keep it be-tween friends,

I know I'll nev - er hold__ you like   I used_ to.
And you don't hold_ me an - y - more.

But a
On

house gets   cold   when you   cut   the heat - ing.   With-out   you_   to hold   I'll   be freez - ing.
cold days   cold   plays out   like   the band's name.   I know   I__   can't heal   things with   a   hand - shake.

Can't   re - ly   on my heart   to beat_   in 'cause you take   parts   of it   ev - 'ry eve - ning.
You know I can   change, as   I   be - gan say - ing. You cut me   wide   o - pen like   land - scape.

U.N.I

Words & Music by Ed Sheeran & Jake Gosling

Now I'm in po - si - tion to be an - oth - er stalk - er like ev - 'ry - thing I say seems to all sound awk - ward.

Like our last kiss,___ it was per - fect,___ we were ner - vous on the sur - face.

Dm

B♭

And I'm al - ways say - ing ev - 'ry - day that it was worth it, pain is on - ly rel - e - vant if it still hurts. I for -

F

D.S. al Coda
(with repeat)

-get like an el - e - phant or we can use a se - da - tive and go back to the day we fell in love on our first kiss.

22

Coda

Whoa._____

Whoa,_____ oh._____ Be-cause_

if I was_ gon-na go some-where, I'd be there by_ now.

And may-be I can let my-self down._____ Whoa._

23

Grade 8

Words & Music by Ed Sheeran, Robert Conlon
& Sukhdeep Uppal

strum-ming on my heart strings like you were a grade 8, but I've nev-er felt this way. I'll pick your feet

___ up off of the ground and nev-er, ev-er let you down, now. You're

strum-ming on my heart strings like you were a grade 8, but I never felt this way. I'll pick your feet

___ up off of the ground and nev-er, ev-er let you down, now.

To Coda ⊕

Wake Me Up

Words & Music by Ed Sheeran & Jake Gosling

Small Bump

Words & Music by Ed Sheeran

44

This

Words & Music by Gordon Mills & Ed Sheeran

The City

Words & Music by Ed Sheeran & Jake Gosling

Lego House

Words & Music by Ed Sheeran, Christopher Leonard
& Jake Gosling

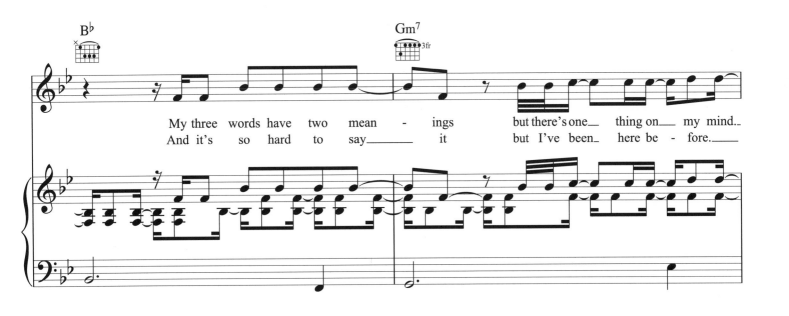

My three words have two mean - ings but there's one__ thing on__ my mind..
And it's so hard to say_____ it but I've been__ here be - fore.____

__ It's all for_____ you, mm._____
__ Now I'll sur - ren - der up my heart_____ and swap it for yours.__

And it's dark in a cold De - cem - ber, but I've got you to keep me warm.__

And out of all these things I've done, I think I love you bet-ter now.

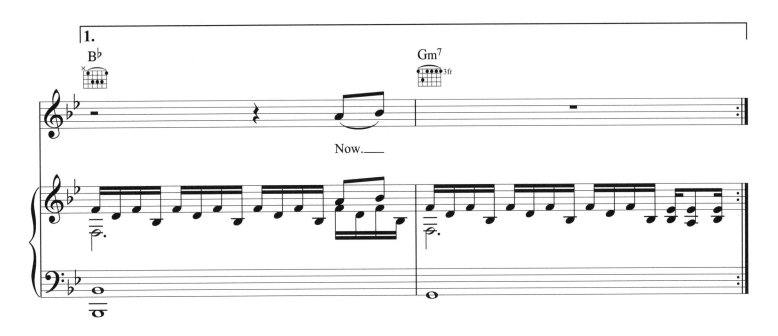

1.

Now.____

2.

Don't hold me down,_____ I think the

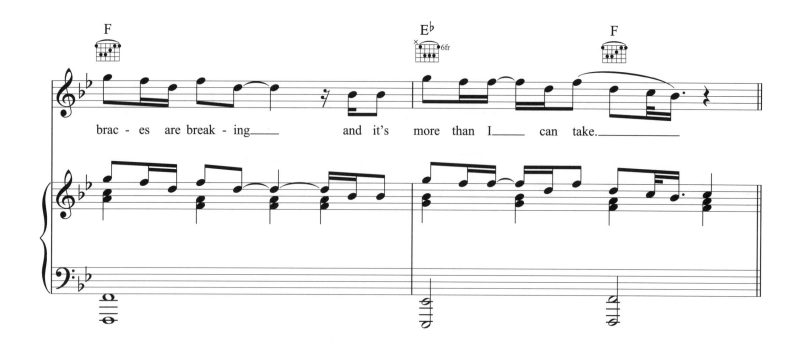

brac - es are break - ing_____ and it's more than I_____ can take._____

And it's dark in a cold De - cem - ber, but I've got you to keep me warm._____

If you're bro - ken, I will mend ya and keep you shel - tered from the storm that's_ rag - ing_ on,_____ now.

I'm out of touch, I'm out of love. I'll pick you up when you're get-ting down.

And out of all these things I've done, I think I love you bet-ter now.

I'm out of sight, I'm out of mind. I'll do it all for you in time.__

And out of all these things I've done, I think I love you bet-ter now.

I'm out of touch, I'm out of love. I'll pick you up when you're get-ting down.

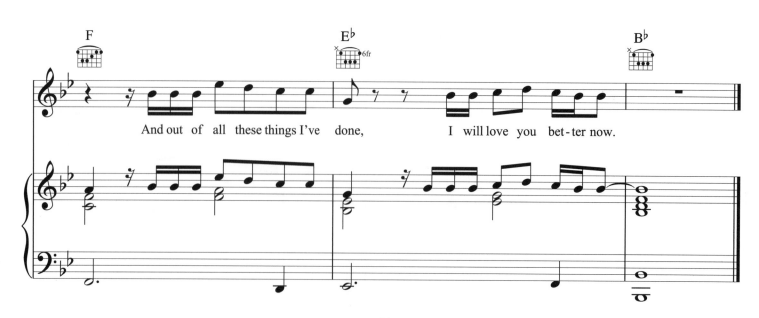

And out of all these things I've done, I will love you bet-ter now.

Kiss Me

Words & Music by Julie Frost, Justin Franks
& Ed Sheeran

loved, you wan - na be_____ loved.

This_____ feels_____ like fall - ing in_____ love,_____ fall - ing in

love, fall-ing in love.___

You Need Me, I Don't Need You

Words & Music by Ed Sheeran

Now I'm in town, break it down. Think-in' of mak-in' a new sound. Play-in' a dif-f'rent show ev-'ry night in front of a new crowd, that's

Give Me Love

Words & Music by Christopher Leonard, Jake Gosling
& Ed Sheeran

'Cause late-ly I've been wak-ing up a- lone.

Paint__ splat - tered tear - drops on my shirt.

Told you I'd let them go. And that I'll

fight my cor-ner. May-be to-night I'll call ya, af - ter my blood__

And that

79

The Parting Glass

Words & Music by Ed Sheeran, Jake Gosling
& Peter Gosling

CONTENTS

MEET THE TEAM

>LEADER

Name: unknown (uses the alias Captain Jack Harkness)
Date of birth: unknown (at least 150) **Status:** former Time Agent, currently in charge of Torchwood Three
Strengths: leadership, charm, apparent immortality
Weaknesses: guarded, has difficulty talking about his past

A one-time con man and former Time Agent, Jack was both redeemed and cursed with eternal life when he was brought back from the space vortex. Since then he has made the most of his endless span of time to become a leader and a hero, preparing the Earth for its turbulent future.

Jack returns to his team newly determined to continue his work at Torchwood alongside his friends. His past continues to catch up with him as former lover Captain John bursts onto the scene **(Kiss Kiss, Bang Bang)**. He is also reminded of the tragic loss of his father and brother **(Adam)**.

At Torchwood Jack has always been particularly close to Gwen and Ianto. While he and Gwen continue to dance around their feelings for each other, his romance with Ianto gathers heat – though sometimes the rest of the team

>CARER

Name: Gwen Cooper
Date of birth: 16/08/78
Status: former police constable, current Torchwood operative
Strengths: empathy, doggedness, strong sense of justice
Weaknesses: stubborn, gets too emotionally involved

When we first met Gwen Cooper, she was an ordinary police constable, albeit a particularly inquisitive one. Then she heard the name Jack Harkness, and her world was never the same again.

After Jack went away, Gwen used her newfound strength and confidence to lead the team in his absence, and decided to commit to Rhys when he asked her to marry him **(Kiss Kiss, Bang Bang)**.

Gwen's world is once again turned upsidedown when Rhys discovers the real nature of her job **(Meat)**. She refuses to give him Jack's amnesia pill, choosing instead to let Rhys remember what he has seen, bringing the couple closer than ever. In true Torchwood style Gwen and Rhys' special day is somewhat disrupted when Gwen almost gives birth to an alien, but

>OFFICE BOY   >DOCTOR   >TECHNICIAN

Name: Ianto Jones **Date of birth:** 02/12/82
Status: current Torchwood operative
Strengths: precision, best coffee this side of the Rift
Weaknesses: secrecy, stopwatches

When we first met Ianto, he was little more than a caretaker/coffee maker, and the public face of the Hub's Tourist Information façade. But over time he has won the confidence of his friends and in joining the team on field assignments continues to prove himself as a more than worthy member of the team.

Ianto is a longstanding Torchwood employee, having worked for Torchwood One in London as a junior researcher before its destruction. He then sort out Torchwood Three in Cardiff. Initially Jack refused to give him a job, but after Ianto helped him fight a Weevil and capture a pterodactyl, Jack was eventually persuaded that he was an essential member of the team **(Fragments)**. Since then he has taken their rela-

Name: Owen Harper **Date of birth:** 14/02/80
Status: current Torchwood operative and medic
Strengths: passionate, brilliant doctor and pathologist
Weaknesses: women, sarcasm, shooting the boss

Owen Harper, "That's Doctor Owen Harper" **(Everything Changes)** and he's not afraid who knows it. Confident in both his work and personal life, Owen can come across as a shallow womaniser, but his experiences with Torchwood have forced him to face up to his deeper emotions.

Owen is shot and killed **(Reset)**, and following a resurrection of sorts he is forced to live a strange animated life where he cannot eat, sleep or have sex. Deprived of all the things he lived for previously, Owen struggles to cope with his new state. However, he proves his mettle to the team, even after his demise, when he literally faces death and fights it, succeeding in banishing it, saving the world and restoring an aging Martha

Name: Toshiko Sato **Date of birth:** 18/09/81
Status: current Torchwood operative
Strengths: logical, cool-headed, determined
Weaknesses: lacks confidence, unlucky in love

Toshiko 'Tosh' Sato may be the most serious-minded of the Torchwood team, but her quiet reserve hides an acid sense of humour and a relentless determination to solve any problem. Her personal life has always taken a back seat to her work, but her capacity for deep feeling is revealed in her relationship with Tommy, a soldier from 1918 who has to be reanimated once a year **(To the Last Man)**. She also adores Owen from afar, finally declaring her love after his death **(Dead Man Walking)**.

The team relies on Tosh's technical experience for a multitude of specialised difficulties. Before her time at Torchwood she used her skills to try to save her mother from her captors. She ended up imprisoned herself, until Jack came to her rescue,

Black Water

By Steven Savile

"**S**omething's changing out there," Tosh said. "Look." She pointed out beyond the dock. She was right. Something was happening out on the black water. While they watched, the sea rippled slickly. The moonlight lay like a silver film stretched taut across its surface. A dozen old boats, rust-pitted fishing tubs and a single pond-hopper ferry, bobbed on their moorings. The midnight tide had them straining against their anchor chains, wanting to draw them out to sea. For a full minute the only sounds in Cardiff Bay were the grind of iron on iron and the gentle slosh of the ebbing tide retreating.

Tosh finished taking the water sample and capped the phial. She sealed it with a twist and slipped it inside her pocket.

It was difficult to make out anything beyond the mouth of the bay because of the night mists rising up off the water. For the last hour they had been rising and thickening, and now they were a solid wall of white that swallowed the dockside apartment blocks and the skeletal frames of the cranes. The phenomenon was not all that uncommon given the time of year; if it wasn't industrial smog being belched out by the factories, it was a natural one choking the city. The mists were caused by a freak collaboration of trapped thermals and shifting weather patterns. What was decidedly more curious was the oily texture of the mist itself and the way the black water seemed to writhe beneath the touch of the moon. It was as though it had a life of its own.

They had picked up the peculiar distress call three hours earlier. The captain's voice had been every bit as desperate as his message warranted. His garbled plea, looping over and over, promised to damn them all. *The Dread* was sailing into the bay ablaze, her cargo: 242 tons of oil in the hull. If she burned, they all would. The man begged over and over for fire crews to be ready to fight the blaze and for the docks to be evacuated. The last transmission closed with the words: "*God help us... We are going to burn...*" and then there was only silence and the occasional burst of static.

It had taken Tosh less than a minute to be sure that *The Dread* wasn't on any of the shipping manifests, and a minute more to trace the last time she had been — according to the archival reports it had been 111 years since *The Dread* had burned out of existence five miles off the headland. When the fires finally died there had been nothing left. The intense heat had consumed the metal, the fires were fed by the oil in her belly so *The Dread* burned and burned until there was nothing left to burn.

That didn't mean they weren't about to take all the necessary precautions tonight. Far from it. The coastguard scrambled an Atlantic 404 Sniffer — the aircraft's remote sensors were capable of detecting spillage beneath the sea's surface. The readings it reported made no sense at all. According to the sensors 111,000 tons of crude oil had amassed around the mouth of the bay, but there was no ship for over 120 miles. The trucks of the fire brigade lined the docks, ready, though no one was sure quite what to expect, or what they could do if the worst actually happened and a fireball sailed into the harbour.

"Here she comes," Jack said, as the prow of a ghost ship emerged slowly from the mist. She was majestic; a huge powerful old steamer, three funnels belching more black smoke up into the air.

They held their breath, waiting, but there were no flames.

Sailing the midnight tide, *The Dread* was a wraith on the black water.

"Right on time," Owen said, looking at his watch. It was eleven minutes past midnight. More black oily mist wreathed the rusted hull of the huge old ship.

"*The Dread*," Jack said. "We're looking at one of the first serious ecological disasters — with a payload of 242 tons of kerosene oil, she burned for six days. The oil wiped out tens of thousands of birds over a 120 mile stretch of the coastline; complete populations of cormorants, guillemots, razorbills, puffins and kittiwakes gone."

"And now she's here," Owen said.

"Which can't be good," Gwen added, as the 404 completed another fly-over.

Tosh looked down at the results scrolling across the small screen of her PDA. "It's amazing," she said. "They're still not picking up any sign of *The Dread* on their scanners. Looking at these results I'd stake my life on the fact that she isn't actually there."

"It's a safe bet that she isn't," Jack said. "At least not *The Dread* that burned off the bay. This could be an echo we're seeing, or it could be something else entirely, but I'm fairly sure that it isn't a ghost."

Even from a distance, at almost 200-feet long, the tanker dwarfed every other vessel in Cardiff Bay.

"So what is it then?"

"Oil," Tosh said, staring at the water.

"What?"

"That's all the Sniffer's scanners are picking up, thousands of tons of oil. There's nothing else out there."

"Well, nothing apart from an enormous great ship that might or might not be about to burst into flames," Owen said.

"Look at the water," Gwen pointed as she spoke. They could all see it, the black sheen rippling beneath the moonlight.

"Looks like oil to me," Ianto said. He wrapped his arms around himself, warding off the chill that had crept into the night.

"Tosh, I want you to get that water checked out," Jack said, rousing the team into action. "I want to know exactly what's in it. Ianto, you're my man on the ground. I want you liaising with the fire services. If this thing goes up we're in trouble. Owen, Gwen, you're coming with me."

They watched *The Dread* glide slowly closer to the dock, the great hulk all the more sinister for the mist rising up off the black water.

"Can you see anyone on the bridge?" Gwen asked, straining to make out anything beyond dark shadows and smears of inky black reflecting back off the blind windows. It took her a moment to realise there were no lights anywhere on the ship, though the occasional flicker of angry red through chinks in the black hinted at a blaze barely contained beneath the surface.

"Doesn't look like anyone's home," Jack said.

"I really don't like the look of this," Gwen murmured, shivering.

It was dark as they descended into the belly of *The Dread*. The darkness was claustrophobic and dizzying, and when the door closed behind them, complete. There was a smell to it that Jack couldn't quite place, not at first. He moved down the narrow stairs carefully, each step testing the darkness, and expecting the world to fall away beneath him.

It didn't.

Instead, at the foot of the stairs it rushed up to meet him unexpectedly. Jack lurched forward, reaching out to catch himself. The world shrank around him until it was no larger than the reach of his arm. He found the wall.

Within a few short moments the ship had earned its name.

There was no hint of the dark relenting, and no reason that it should.

"Okay, it's dark. That's a drag but it doesn't mean we're helpless. We've got five senses — it's time to start using them," Jack said. The darkness had a curious dampening effect on his voice. He was right though, just because they couldn't see, that didn't mean they couldn't hear, touch, taste or smell what was waiting for them. Indeed he had already touched the wall, however accidental the contact had been. The fact he hadn't fallen through it pretty much negated the notion of it being ectoplasmic or in any way ethereal.

Jack rubbed his fingers against the heel of his palm. There was some sort of greasy residue all over them.

The ghost ship neither creaked nor groaned as it moved with the gentle sway of the water. The silence was every bit as unnatural as the all-consuming black that gathered around them. There should have been so many more little noises, from the thrum of the engines down below to the *tick tick tick* cooling of the metal walls and the muffled clang of their footsteps on the metal floor. But the darkness was silent.

Even as he realised that all of the other sounds were missing, Jack sensed Owen fumbling beside him, and guessed he was about to pull out his torch. Jack stopped him with a single word: "Oil."

The smell of it was all around them. It was all-pervasive. Invasive. It cloyed in the throat and burned in the nostrils as he breathed. The sensation of it clawing its way into his lungs was vile. Beside him, Gwen started coughing, trying to purge her body of the reek. He felt it niggling away inside his head. Jack rested the flat of his hand against the partition wall. Part of him wanted to flinch instinctively; it felt so utterly wrong. It took him a moment to realise what was missing. The wall felt wet, sticky — that explained the residue on his fingers — and as he pushed tentatively against it, seemed to melt around his hand, not completely, there was still some resistance, but more than any sort of metal should. But that wasn't it. There were no vibrations from the engine room.

Beside him, there was a sharp snap as Owen broke a glow-stick and the corridor was suffused immediately with a soft phosphorescent green glow. Owen smirked at him, his face transformed into a death's head mask by the unnatural light. "Do I look like an idiot? Second thoughts, don't answer that."

He held the glow-stick out, lighting their way.

The ship's corridor ran away in front of them, branching off twice before the faint glow finally gave the shapes back to shadow. Jack walked side by side with Owen to the first intersection. The details were sloppy. They were there, all the decals and the piping, the rivet work and the rubber seals, but they were all... lacking... as though their sharp edges had slipped slightly under the heat.

Heat.

Jack couldn't believe he'd missed it. It was so obvious but it hadn't occurred to him. He tried to think. To remember exactly what he had seen — flickers of flame, reddish flares of colour against the black night. He had definitely seen them, but there was no answering heat in the super-structure of the ship. The old cliché might have promised no smoke without fire, but there was certainly no fire without heat. And there was no heat. He pressed his hand up against the interior wall again. It was cold to the touch; not even the faintest residual heat.

"What are we looking for?" Gwen asked.

Jack wasn't sure, but it certainly wasn't what they found.

The deeper they went into *The Dread* the more disturbing the tanker became.

Initially it had just been the lack of sound, the peculiar oleaginous texture of the walls, the wax-drip of the contours and the cloying reek that together set Jack's skin to crawling, but the deeper they went the more sinister and unnatural things became. He began to catch glimpses of movement, always out of their peripheral vision, but whenever he tried to chase it down, the corridors and passageways were empty.

He tried eleven doors.

Eleven rooms stood empty, the bunks, like something out of a pre-war fever hospital, were all neatly made. Nothing was out of place in any of the abandoned bunk rooms. Jack stepped into the twelfth room. It was just like the others, steeped in dank institutional air, everything laid out just so. He looked down at the bed. The sheets were folded tight with hospital corners. The flat pillow caught his eye. He made to move it, but it was fused to the rest of the bed. Puzzled, Jack tried to pull back at the sheets, but they didn't move; like the pillow they were actually a part of the mattress. The rest of the room was the same, the gilt frame of the oil painting on the wall was inseparable from the wall it hung on, the metal legs of the bed frame and the bedside table rose up seamlessly from the floor.

He backed out of the room.

The passageway was the same, he realised.

"I want to check something out," Jack said to the others, changing direction. He had been on enough ships in his time to know they all more or less followed a basic layout. He led them to the mess hall, and then through to the galley. Just like in the bunk room everything was somehow fused to everything else, right down to the plates and cutlery, the hanging pots and the racks of tinned food.

"Take one," he said, nodding toward what looked like a can of peaches. Gwen tried. "It's like that everywhere, every piece of furniture, every fork and spoon, even the pictures on the walls, they're all part of the ship."

"That's just weird," Gwen said, looking at the can that refused to move.

"So we're not talking about a ghost ship then?" Owen asked, trying for himself.

They carried on searching, finding everything except for people. There were countless signs of life fused into the hulk of the tanker, but the signs lead nowhere.

The engine rooms were the worst; pistons moved, gliding up and down effortlessly — and silently. Steam vented, again without a sound. Everything that ought to have been a cacophony on a working ship was performed by *The Dread* in complete silence.

When the steam touched the wall it melded back into it flawlessly.

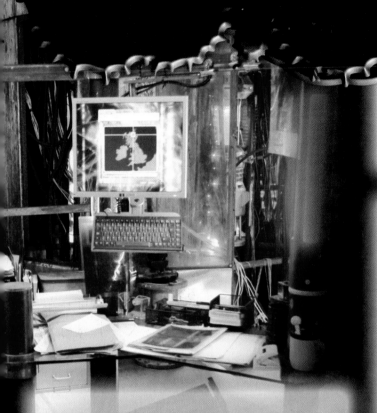

they needed to contain it, then they could move towards eradicating the threat it posed.

She picked up the phone to call Ianto. He needed to know.

Ianto stood on the dock, digesting what Tosh had just told him.

He killed the earpiece with a single press and tried to reach Jack to let him know. There was nothing. No signal.

There was movement down on the ship. He squinted towards it, trying to make out who was moving about topside, but it was impossible to tell. For a moment, a trick of the darkness and moonlight perhaps, it looked as though the figures had no features. When they looked towards him he saw plain empty faces. The moonlight slivered across them like an oily wash.

"No fire," Ianto said to the man beside him. "There's a chemical compound in the oil that means we can't just burn it out. Whatever happens, that tanker can't be allowed to burn."

"Understood," the fire chief said. He relayed the message to his crew, and they in turn sent it on to the coastguard. *The Dread* would not be allowed to burn.

Ianto walked down toward the gangplank where a figure was shuffling off the ship. The sailor moved clumsily, dragging his feet.

"You! Wait!" Ianto called, trying to catch the man's attention as he hurried down to meet him.

The sailor turned, and in that moment Ianto knew it was no illusion. Features grew out of the face as he stared, horrified, watching the figure — whatever it was — mimic his face.

Somewhere in the distance a forlorn foghorn cried out into the night.

The mimic reached out for Ianto, stumbling forward. Its mirror-mouth opened and closed over and over soundlessly. The copy was perfect, scarily so. It was only the eyes that betrayed it; they were dead, filled with black oil.

"Oh, no," Ianto said, pulling away before it could touch him. "I don't think so."

But it wasn't him it was staggering toward; the figure lumbered towards the fire engine even as more of the creatures emerged from the belly of the ship, seeming to pull out of the rust-pitted hull in some grotesque parody of birth.

It took him a moment to realise what they were trying to do.

They were being drawn towards the vehicles.

It was their instinct to spread far and wide.

Tosh stared at the results coming through from the analysis.

The first flow of numbers covered optical density, wavelength analysis of photon absorption and a particulate breakdown. Together these could be used to determine what was natural Cardiff Bay bilge and any newly-introduced contaminants. Curious, she put the sample into a centrifugal separator to sift out the impurities.

What she was left with bore a remarkable resemblance to crude petroleum, though the balance of hydrocarbons was off — too many large hydrocarbons and too few small ones for it to be a good fuel. Breaking it down with a hot catalyst would change things though.

There was something else too; a compound unlike anything she had seen before. It didn't match anything from the known periodic table, meaning it was almost certainly non-terrestrial. That was something she could work with.

Over the next hour she ran a series of experiments. The results did nothing to comfort her.

She studied the sample under the electron microscope and the spectrometer. The alien compound reacted aggressively against anything introduced to the water, breaking it down and stripping it of its vital energy until all that remained was a sludge not unlike bitumin. What was more interesting was what happened to the compound itself: it became energised, flourishing as it devoured the reagent. The element was a parasite. It fed on the filth of the water and defended itself with crude intelligence.

When she heated the sample the entire process went to Hell. It didn't just crack to form fuel, there was some kind of catalyst in the water itself that meant when exposed to heat it multiplied exponentially. The thing was voracious. In a matter of minutes it had doubled in size again to fill the slide. A minute later it was eating into the glass. She watched it for a full five minutes more, horrified by the black water's appetite. One thing she knew for sure: trying to burn the oil away would be a disaster.

It was using the Rift to search for new matter to absorb, not just here and now on Earth but through space and time.

There has to be a compound that will counteract the growth, she thought. That is the way science works. Something out there would degrade the hydrocarbons and break down whatever the alien element was. First

It was only when the black water came into contact with the base unit that Tosh realised the true extent of the threat. The black oily goo changed when it reached the mechanism inside. It coiled around the cables, stripping them bare, and began to eat into the electrics. Or so it appeared at first — but the wiring didn't corrode or fray.

Moving instinctively, she snatched the plug from the wall, isolating the contagion inside the microscope. The cable

lashed back and forth on the ceramic floor for a moment before falling still.

A second later and it would have been out into the main grid, free to go anywhere, feeding on the power surging through the lines that carried it.

If not exactly sentient, the black water had a purpose: to spread. It reacted to an alien presence with what could only be called a self-defence mechanism. The question was, was it instinctive, reactive, or did it imply some sort of driving thought?

Tosh considered all the things in the world that relied upon oil to power them, and how helpless the entire planet would become if the contagion were allowed to spread into the oil supply and taint it with its hunger. From plastics formed out of petroleum through every petroleum-based product, to the very oil that fired the heating and fuelled cars and gave us electricity, it was everywhere in everyday life.

Hell, oil was king.

Wars had been fought under the pretence of owning it, controlling its flow, because it was that important in the modern world. The notion that the black water might have a purpose beyond simple self-preservation sent a shiver down the ladder of her spine.

She couldn't prove that the stuff was capable of conscious thought, not yet, but she strongly suspected that it was. Everything pointed to it. The compound had shied away from the reagent aimed at breaking it down, and followed a line of least resistance to the first outlet to the power grid. That, if anything, had to be evidence of at least basic intelligence. It followed its primary instinct — to reproduce.

But its strength is also its weakness, Tosh realised, the beginnings of a plan forming.

Unable to reach Jack, she called Ianto. What he told her confirmed all of her worst fears. The oil was separating from the 'ghost ship' and looking for ways into power lines, petrol tanks and any other chance to seep into the national grid. That it had the ability to mimic humanity though, that she hadn't expected.

Jack, Gwen and Owen were in trouble.

Jack noticed it first; the machines were losing their consistency and melting into the rest of the ship's innards, as though *The Dread* were collapsing in on itself.

"We've got to get out! Fast!"

But fast wasn't enough — the melting engines had been a distraction. Five 'bodies' began to take shape, tearing gradually free of the walls. As they pulled forward, the walls stretched, the illusion of the engine room breaking as the black oil leaked through the cracks, dribbling down like tears. For a moment the bodies had been amorphous, formless, but as they tore free soundlessly they began to take on features of their own, mirroring the faces of the Torchwood team they grappled with.

It wasn't a fair fight. Jack twisted and lashed out, but their oily foes simply absorbed the blows, showing no signs of any pain. More and more arms reached out of the wall and floor, dragging them bodily into the ooze of the melting ship as it closed in around them.

And it wasn't only oil that leaked in through *The Dread*'s breached walls.

Black water rose up around their legs as the engine room flooded. Only now did sounds start to infiltrate the sickly green dark, bubbling in with the water. As though hearing them gave her permission, Gwen screamed.

If they didn't suffocate from being engulfed by the melting walls, they would almost certainly drown within a matter of minutes. Jack wasn't scared for himself — he could metaphorically hold his breath for an eternity — but Owen and Gwen couldn't.

Already it was cold. So cold.

They couldn't run. And as they were sucked into the hulk of *The Dread* they couldn't breathe.

Time was the one thing they didn't have.

The Dread was collapsing.

The 404 flew low, trailing white powder in its wake.

"Are you sure this is going to work?" Ianto asked sceptically.

Tosh nodded, watching the vapour trails. "It's petroleum based. They're spraying a bio-remedial agent over everything. It's a simple enough idea — the micro-organisms in the powder basically eat through the hydrocarbons of the petroleum, degrading it to the point that it's clean water. The waste leaks into the air as carbon-dioxide. It's been developed for cleaning up oil spills and protecting the wildlife. It's got to work," she said, more a prayer than a promise.

"If you say so," Ianto said, no more convinced than he had been a minute before. He sprinkled the sailor that had stolen his face with handfuls of the powder; the sailor's 'skin' bubbled and hissed as it was quickly reduced to a puddle of ooze on the grass, the powder corroding through it as it came into contact with the water that made up so much of its form. A moment later the ooze started to soak up into the powder, leaving the grass damp but clean.

The white powder settled across the surface of the bay, thickening like snow as it clung to the black water.

"Where are they?"

The central funnel of the tanker crumbled, caving in on itself. The black oil leaked out across the rippling surface, only to be soaked up by the white powder. More and more of the bulkhead began to collapse, the tanker leaking thick black oil out into the bay as more white powder fell from the sky.

And still there was no sign of Jack or the others.

"They're dead, aren't they?" Ianto said, sickly. He knew it, down in his heart. He knew it.

"No," Tosh said, slipping an arm around his waist and drawing him in to an embrace. The two of them stood there for a long time, watching the water for any sign of the others.

And then, in the middle of the bay, they saw movement.

The air broke around Jack's head. He came up to the surface, gasping. He was clutching Gwen to him. Owen came up next, covered from head to toe in the black stuff.

It didn't matter one little bit.

They were alive. ▨

GRAND DESIGNS

CENTRAL TO THE LOOK AND FEEL OF TORCHWOOD, THE HUGE AND IMPOSING HUB IS THE WORK OF PRODUCTION DESIGNER **EDWARD THOMAS** AND SERIES DESIGNER **JULIAN LUXTON**. IN THIS SECTION, JULIAN GUIDES US THROUGH THE ELEMENTS THAT MAKE UP THE SET, WHILE ON PAGE 20, EDWARD TALKS ABOUT HOW IT ALL BEGAN...

THE UPPER DECK

"When we were designing the Hub for series one, we decided to make it a 360-degree set, because we didn't want to limit the visual possibilities of filming any part of it. But in so doing, we did slightly limit where the cameras could shoot from. So this year we've extended the deck level a bit further, and added some more levels and some more manoeuvrability. Using the depth of the Hub worked really well in the first series, so we're just emphasising that, really."

THE TOWER

"When we first started thinking about the tower in the bay, we realised how rooted into the ground it looked, so we knew it would have to come all the way down!"

THE WATER

"The great thing about water is the reflections it gives: you can use it to create wonderful lighting effects. But it's an important design feature too, because it does show that behind that dam is Cardiff Bay. That wall is holding out the Bay, and it leaks! That's why it's tidal. Also, it gets away from the idea that you're in a studio, with clean, flat floors. Directors might not like us for it, but we just don't do flat floors!"

THE HOTHOUSE

"We decided this year that there should be somewhere the team could use as a quiet area, where they could have time alone, or talk on a one-to-one basis. So with the old boardroom vacant, we started to think about what would look good – and what could be better than alien flowers? It makes things visually more interesting, and it adds some colour, as well as making it feel a little more private and secluded, like a sci-fi potting shed."

WORKSTATIONS

"There's always a lot of personal detail on the workstations, because the guys who dress our sets live it for real. They know the mythology, and they know how to use all that knowledge in a sympathetic way. They take great pride in what they do, and nothing ever gets put there for the sake of it. Even the paperwork on the desks is written out in full, not just because we're shooting in HD, but because it makes it as real as possible for everyone involved."

Inside the hothouse

Dalek guns in the Armoury

"The armoury was always meant to be a fast-response unit. The red doors lead through to a garage area, so the team can tool up and hit the road. Sadly, we've never needed to show the garage, but I'd love to build it one day. The guns are a combination of real ballistic weaponry and alien tech from Doctor Who. There's more in there this year, so we've added a middle section of hanging racks with Dalek guns on, which Torchwood salvaged from 1930s New York."

THE DAM WALL

"We designed sections of the dam wall to be removable, so the cameras could get quite far back and shoot into the Hub from a distance. Originally, we were going to add to the dragon painting (pictured below) throughout series one, but we realised it would be a nightmare for continuity!"

Toshiko's workstation

The dragon on the dam wall

THE BOARDROOM

"We blew up the boardroom at the end of series one, which gave us the opportunity to do something new this year. So we came up with a design for a new boardroom, the idea being that it's inside a big pipe, somewhere in the depths of the Hub, which the team converted to suit their requirements. By putting it down there, we can also get down-the-line shots through the tunnels, which really adds depth and brings it to life."

THE DOOR

"When the Hub was built, that door would have been part of a big outlet pump in a huge docking area for ships and submarines. But when that section collapsed and the modern concrete wall was put in, they salvaged the door and reused it for defensive purposes. Along with the cage, it makes for a good alien trap. It's a solid piece of Victorian engineering!"

THE MORGUE

"The mortuary was designed to have that incredibly impressive Victorian look, albeit with modern adaptations. It was intended to hold an army of aliens if necessary, and it's been there, pretty much unchanged, throughout Torchwood's history.

There are only two real elements to the morgue: an arch at the front, and a section of the drawers, with the rest done in CGI. But we've designed it in such a way that we can add to it, and this year we've got some more matte paintings, so you can see the whole length of these giant cold storage areas."

JACK'S OFFICE

"Jack is a mystery, really. He has his own ways and his own tech that he's been accumulating over the years, as well as some elements from his former life as a Time Agent. We put some things in which we never thought people would pick up on, like the fact that he's growing a TARDIS out of coral on his desk. But then the writers get to hear about those things, and suddenly they appear in a script!

"Another example of that is the televisions, which are scanning the Rift for RF signals from the past or the future. It's never elaborated on, but those TVs came from Magpie's shop, where they were linked to The Wire [in the Doctor Who episode The Idiot's Lantern], and Jack isn't going to let that alien technology go to waste."

JACK'S BUNK

"Russell always wanted Jack to live in the Hub, but not necessarily have a full-on bedroom. We know from Doctor Who and hints about his military past that he's used to sleeping in vehicles and barracks, so the idea of an underground bunk with a submarine-style hatch seemed to fit that. I think we've only ever seen him down there once."

THE AUTOPSY ROOM

"This was originally one of several refrigerated areas along the railway platform, so you could get aliens off the train and straight in to cold storage. There are shafts under the autopsy room, with a lift mechanism that leads into the mortuary area. So you can examine things, then send them off for storage more long term."

BASE INSTINCTS

TORCHWOOD PRODUCTION DESIGNER **EDWARD THOMAS** ON THE INSPIRATIONS FOR THE HUB, AND HOW IT FOUND A HOME IN CARDIFF BAY.

"**R**USSELL WAS VERY NON-SPECIFIC ABOUT the Hub in the first script for Torchwood, as he was with the TARDIS on Doctor Who," says Edward Thomas about Torchwood creator and executive producer Russell T Davies. "That's great for us as an art department, because it means he trusts us to get it right, but we didn't know if it should be a factory unit, a bunker, or what. We just knew it needed to be beautiful and sexy.

"So we started talking about which areas of Cardiff would give us the most beautiful exteriors, and, of course, you don't have to be a genius to realise that the Bay gives you all that in one place. And once you start looking at it, all centred around that sculpture, you think, what the hell is that thing? Well, in our eyes it could only ever be an alien transmitter! It was never just a piece of art.

"After that, we went down there on a recce with a couple of concept artists and set designers, and who do we see, but Russell, who was out buying milk or something. We'd just discovered the area for the exterior of the tourist information office, so we were able to stop him then and there and say, 'This is what we're thinking about: there's the tower, the base is underneath, it comes out here, what do you think?' And he absolutely loved it, and went straight back home and started writing for it!

"We tried to make the Hub as visually exciting as we could, with all those layers of Victoriana and contemporary modernism, to reflect the history of the organisation. Just as scripts have many layers, it's our job to put many layers into the sets. We have to address the balance between the practical and the visually amazing, but sometimes visually amazing wins!

"The great thing about working on these shows is that everybody cares about it, from the top down. The Hub is so detailed that it's almost like a museum in some places, which most sets aren't. You see them in real life and it is just a piece of wood. But the Hub is real and it was built to last. It's a very unusual set by anyone's standards." ▓

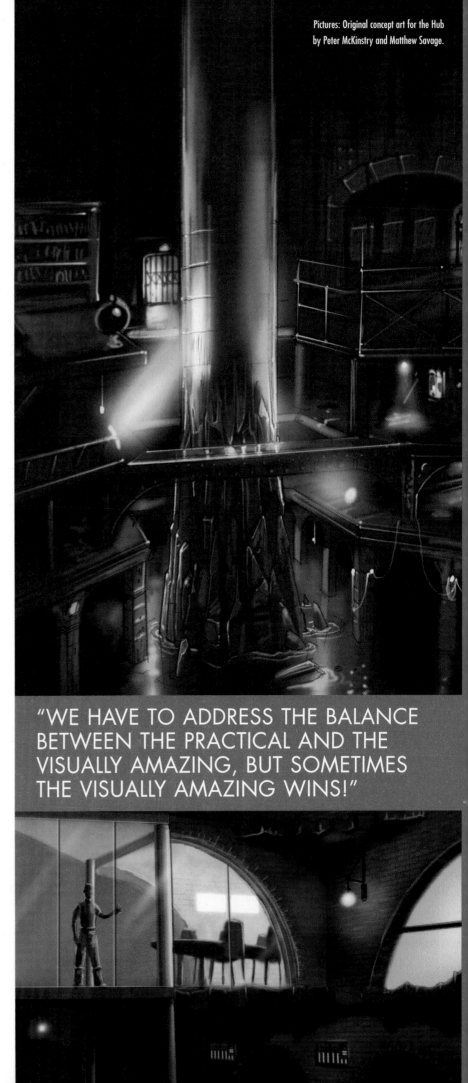

Pictures: Original concept art for the Hub by Peter McKinstry and Matthew Savage.

"WE HAVE TO ADDRESS THE BALANCE BETWEEN THE PRACTICAL AND THE VISUALLY AMAZING, BUT SOMETIMES THE VISUALLY AMAZING WINS!"

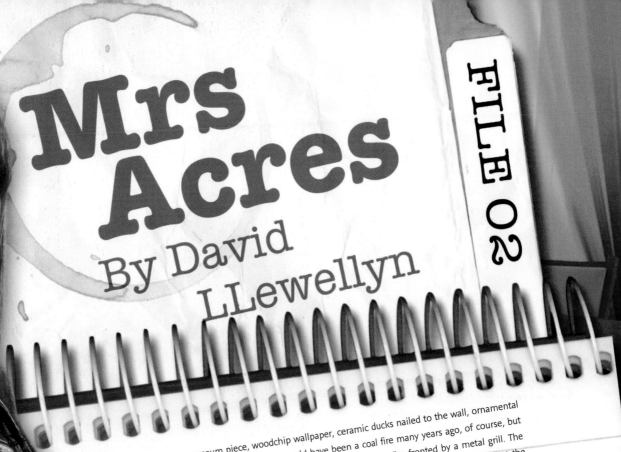

Mrs Acres

By David Llewellyn

The house was a museum piece, woodchip wallpaper, ceramic ducks nailed to the wall, ornamental dogs either side of the fireplace. There would have been a coal fire many years ago, of course, but that had long since been replaced with an ugly bright-purple gas fire fronted by a metal grill. The television was a Grundig, the screen of which bulged out from its frame and was rounded at the corners. There were antimacassars on the armchairs, and Catherine Cookson novels on the bookshelves. The grandfather clock in the hallway ticked and tocked. The whole place smelled of lavender oil.

Lavender oil and cats.

Mrs Acres entered the living room carrying a jangling tea tray, on which sat an ancient-looking teapot, two cups, and a small plate of Jaffa Cakes.

"There you go, Miss Cooper," she said, placing the tray on the largest table that she'd pulled out from a nest in the far corner. "I hope Jaffa Cakes are okay. I've run out of chocolate digestives."

"No," Gwen smiled politely, "that's lovely, thanks."

This was going to be, Gwen decided, one of *those* afternoons. She imagined the others were having all sorts of adventures. They had probably solved the mystery already and were, no doubt, back at the Hub and laughing at her expense. She pictured some bizarre creature, the prime suspect in their investigation, snarling and spitting behind the reinforced glass of one of the cells.

"Terrible business, mind." Mrs Acres eased herself into a tired-looking armchair, and rested one bandaged foot on a threadbare pouffe.

"Yes," Gwen agreed, sipping her tea and nodding.

The excitement of their journey to this part of the city now seemed a distant memory. Ianto had been up front with Jack, as was often the case these days, reading out the details from his PDA.

"Fourteen cats and eight dogs."

"But only pets?" Owen had asked, "Only animals?"

"So far, yes," continued Ianto.

"A fox?" Gwen had volunteered. "You get loads of city foxes these days."

"What about a chupacabra?" suggested Toshiko.

"Isn't that a type of lollypop?" deadpanned Owen.

"The goatsucker!" Jack laughed. "Chupacabra. But there's never been a recorded case in the UK."

"What about another dog?" asked Owen. "I mean, sorry to micturate on everyone's chips and all, but..."

"It would have to be some dog," Ianto interrupted. "It bit the head off a 126-pound Rottweiler."

And now Gwen was here, in Mrs Acres' living room, drinking tea and eating Jaffa Cakes.

"Mrs Phillips only lost her husband in January," continued the old woman. "She hadn't had that dog three months. Lovely little thing, he was. Little West Highland Terrier. You'd see her walking him in the mornings. Used to take him all the way over to Roath Park, and with *her* hip."

In the hallway the clock filled the silence. *Tick. Tock.*

"I remember when they found him. It was one of the boys three doors up. He was out in the lane with his friends and they found him."

Mrs Acres shook her head dolefully.

"Terrible thing," she sighed.

The team had split up on their arrival in Splott. Toshiko had drawn up a map of the area, highlighting the streets where pets had been attacked or killed. The attacks formed a cluster around this one street — Courtenay Road — and so they'd separated and gone door to door.

"Like salesmen," Owen had joked, "or Jehovah's Witnesses."

The others, Gwen imagined, had escaped lightly. Houses where the individual members of Torchwood were mistaken for debt collectors or, as Owen had said, salesmen. Residents who had little information to offer. Gwen had already been to three such houses before arriving at Mrs Acres' front door.

"I didn't grow up around here, though," said the old woman, apropos of nothing. "Not in Cardiff. I grew up in The Valleys. Up Rhondda way. You get used to seeing things like that up there. I remember one time coming home from school and my aunty was skinning rabbits in the scullery. You've never seen such a thing in your life. It was like a bloodbath!"

She chuckled softly, shaking her head.

"But here? In Cardiff? I saw the look on that boy's face. He was white as a sheet. Heaven knows what he saw."

Gwen took another sip of her tea. It was strong, like the tea her grandmother always made. It tasted different from the tea she drank anywhere else, and Gwen wondered, with a wry smile that she hid behind the teacup, whether there was a special shop where old women bought their tea.

"Of course, a thing like this gets the gossips' tongues a-wagging," said Mrs Acres, raising a disapproving eyebrow as she lifted her cup to her lips. "Never happier than when there's some sort of scandal."

"Mm," murmured Gwen, nodding and biting a Jaffa Cake into the shape of a crescent moon.

"Are you married, Miss Cooper?" asked Mrs Acres. Then she laughed and shook her head.

"*Miss* Cooper! And there's me asking you if you're married."

"That's okay," said Gwen. "I'm engaged, actually."

Mrs Acres beamed.

"Oh, that's lovely," she said. "So many young couples nowadays don't bother. They just move in together. There's nothing wrong with that, of course, but it's such a shame they don't think there's anything special about that commitment, that promise."

Gwen looked around the room again. She'd suddenly realised that there were no photographs anywhere in the house. So many other things reminded her of her grandmother's house, only her grandmother's house was practically bursting at the seams with old photographs. Photographs of Gwen's mother, her aunties and uncles, Gwen and her cousins when they were children. There were school photographs and wedding photographs. Portraits of stoic Edwardians with glassy eyes. Mrs Acres had no photographs.

"And... what about... Mr Acres?" asked Gwen, wording it as sensitively as she could.

"He passed," said Mrs Acres, smiling softly at Gwen. "A long time ago, in Korea.

1951. People tend to forget we went over there, too."

Somewhere in the house Gwen heard footsteps — across the landing, and then down the stairs. Heavy, thumping footsteps, and the sound of somebody, a man, loudly blowing his nose.

"Oh, don't mind him," said Mrs Acres, "that's just my son, Colin."

The door of the living room opened, and a tall, heavy-set man in his mid-forties entered the room. He cut a shambolic figure, filling the doorframe, shoulders sloping beneath a knitted tank top, his hair slicked flat in a side parting. He didn't look *old*, as such, just old-fashioned.

Colin looked down at Gwen with a glower, and then across at his mother.

"This is Miss Cooper," said Mrs Acres. "She's just here to talk about what's been going on. With the pets."

Colin looked from his mother to Gwen and back again.

"Foxes, most likely." He spoke, his voice a plodding monotone. "It's the rubbish, see? All these fast food places and people leaving scraps in the gutter. The foxes are coming into the cities."

He turned to Gwen again.

"So are you with the police?"

Gwen shook her head. "Not as such, no."

Colin huffed through his nose and padded across the living room toward the kitchen.

"I'm putting the kettle on. Anyone for a brew?"

"Oh, no thanks, love," said Mrs Acres. "We've only just made a pot."

Gwen heard the sound of cupboard doors opening and closing, the kettle clattering down onto the hob, the scrape of instant coffee granules being scooped out of a jar. She wondered whether the others would be back at the Hub yet. She wondered what time Rhys was finishing work. Somewhere, tucked away in her subconscious, there was still a part of her worrying about bridesmaids' dresses and florists.

Multitasking was one thing, but preparations for the wedding were becoming torturous.

"So," said Gwen, "just the two of you, is it?"

Mrs Acres nodded, clasping her cup of tea in both hands and looking out through her window at a sky the colour of soapy water. In the hallway the clock ticked away. In the kitchen the water in the kettle began to bubble.

"Just the two of us, yes," said Mrs Acres. "But we've got each other."

She turned to Gwen.

"Do you have any children?"

Gwen shook her head.

"Oh, God no... Not yet, anyway. No."

"They are a blessing," said Mrs Acres, "most of the time. I never thought I'd have a child, after Mr Acres passed, I mean."

Gwen looked through to the kitchen and saw the awkwardly lumbering semi-giant shuffling towards the fridge. Her first observations were correct. Colin *did* only look forty-five at the very oldest. And Mr Acres had been dead more than fifty years.

"Excuse me for asking," said Gwen, "but how old is Colin?"

"I'm not really sure," replied Mrs Acres, smiling sweetly — that reassuring, good-natured smile that Gwen had gradually become accustomed to. It was a smile that didn't reach her eyes; a smile that only a mother, practised at holding things back, can give.

Gwen leaned forward in her chair.

"I'm sorry?" she asked. "What do you mean?"

"I was a nurse," began Mrs Acres, "at St Helens. Not the new place. The old hospital, I mean. They knocked it down years ago. Mr Acres was playing rugby, fell, sprained his ankle. They brought him into the hospital, and he was all smiles and jokes. We saw each other at a dance a few months later and he asked me out. He was a real charmer."

She laughed and shook her head.

"We were married the next spring. None of this waiting around in those days. We had our honeymoon in Bournemouth, which was a big deal then. Three nights in a hotel on the seafront."

Gwen looked into the kitchen once more. Colin was stirring the coffee in a NO.1 SON mug, but he was staring at her.

"He was in the army, of course, but it wasn't until they gave him his orders that any of that seemed real. I'd never thought they'd send him away like that."

Gwen's attention returned to the old woman. She was still smiling, but now there were tears in her eyes. Just five minutes ago Gwen had wanted nothing more than to finish her tea and leave, but she was beginning to realise that this might not be wise.

"How long were you married?" she asked.

"Eighteen months in all," said Mrs Acres, "not even two years. The photos are in boxes in the attic. I had them up, at first, in frames. But then after a while you realise only one of you is getting any older."

Colin stepped out of the kitchen and edged his way across the living room sideways, to avoid brushing ornaments from the sideboard. He looked down at Gwen again with his piercing green/blue eyes, but whatever animosity Gwen had sensed at first had dissipated. He looked strangely sad.

"I'm just going upstairs," he said.

"Yes, dear," said Mrs Acres.

Colin left the room, and once again the *thud thud thud* of his footsteps traced his journey upstairs. Mrs Acres sighed. "He's a good lad. He's just a little shy around strangers."

In the hallway the grandfather clock chimed half past the hour.

"After Mr Acres passed I trained to become a doctor. It was practically unheard of in those days, nurses becoming doctors. I don't know why I did it. I wanted something more, I suppose. The work, studying and all that, took my mind off other things. It was hard work, but it was worth it.

"I went back to St Helens in 1958, only now I was a doctor. I worked on A and E, paediatrics. I got friendly with some of the research staff there, and worked in the laboratories for a while."

A pause. Mrs Acres gazed down at the surface of her tea before delicately placing her cup back on the tray. Gwen felt her pulse quicken.

"They tested drugs there in those days," continued Mrs Acres. "Medicines and what have you. Right up in the annexe, above all the wards. It spooked me when I first went in there — all those cages, and the sounds of all the animals rattling around inside them.

"I'd been there a few years when they brought it in. A litter of kittens, strays they were, that somebody had found down on the docks. No home to go to, so somebody thought we could use them. Eight little kittens wrapped up in a blanket inside an old banana crate."

Gwen put her teacup back on the tray and it chimed emptily against the edge of its saucer.

"Oh, you've finished your tea," said Mrs Acres. "I'll go and

make another pot."

Gwen raised her hands, ready to turn down the offer, but Mrs Acres was already on her feet, hobbling to keep the weight off her injured leg.

"Did you have an accident?" Gwen asked, gesturing toward the dressing.

"Oh, it was nothing," Mrs Acres replied, "just a scratch."

As the elderly woman made her way to the kitchen Gwen noticed it again. That smell. In her days on the force she and Andy had visited a flat in Grangetown where a woman lived with fifteen cats. The council and the RSPCA had been called in, and the woman had become abusive. The smell wasn't just in the flat itself. From the moment they stepped off the elevator they could smell it, that rank animal stench, permeating every corridor of the building's ninth floor.

Now Gwen could smell it again, but something was wrong. The cat woman's flat had been littered with fur, and almost every item of furniture had been clawed and scratched at some point in its history. More to the point, the cat woman's flat had been full of cats and the evidence of cats: the litter tray near the back door, the bowls of drying food and the saucers of milk. Mrs Acres' house had none of that.

"Do *you* have any pets at all?" Gwen raised her voice so Mrs Acres could hear her.

"Oh, no, dear," replied Mrs Acres. "There's the food to buy, and all the things that go with them."

She returned from the kitchen carrying a tray replenished with tea and cakes. Once she'd handed Gwen her cup and coerced her into eating another cake she sat back in her armchair and let out a long sigh.

"Where was I?" she said. "I'd forget my head if it wasn't screwed on!"

"You were talking about working at the hospital," prompted Gwen, "in the labs."

"Oh yes," said Mrs Acres, her expression saddening. "The kittens."

"They came in a banana crate, all wrapped up in a blanket. One of the other doctors began sorting through them and that's when he came to the runt. The others were all colours: tortoiseshell, black and white. One of them was that kind of blue-grey colour. Do you know what I mean?"

Gwen nodded.

"But the runt," said Mrs Acres, "he was just this little thing, smaller than the others, and not a bit of hair on him. None of us thought he'd last the night, but he did. We fed him milk and kept him wrapped up warm, and every morning I'd go in to check up on him.

"That was when I noticed it."

"What's that?" asked Gwen.

"He'd lost his tail. Oh, it had been there when he came in, but now it was gone. And his paws... His paws were... Well, they were *different*."

"Different... how?"

"They looked like hands. Like little hands. I knew something was wrong but... it was like nothing I'd ever seen before. Every day there was something different; the eyes, the ears. Eventually I decided I had to do something, so I took him from the cage where we kept him and I brought him home."

Mrs Acres looked out of the window again. The clouds that had been gathering all day were now a darker grey.

"I've always thought," she continued, "that maybe it was being around people that changed him; maybe he just copied the things that were around him. The longer he spent with us, the more he looked like us. Now I'm not so sure. It's like whatever's in him that changes, it keeps changing, never settles."

"Colin..." Gwen whispered.

Mrs Acres nodded.

"That's the name I gave him. After Mr Acres. I told the others at the hospital the kitten had died. He'd been so weak, they didn't question it. I told the neighbours he was my nephew, that I'd had a sister who passed away.

"Having him was the best thing that ever happened to me. However much I involved myself in work, it never quite filled the emptiness, but looking after this little thing, this *child*... It was like a gift. Like somebody had given me this amazing gift. I don't know what I would have done without him.

"And now *this*."

Mrs Acres looked at Gwen. Her eyes shone with tears that welled and rolled over the wrinkled contours of her cheeks in thin streams.

"You *are* Torchwood, aren't you?"

Gwen was shocked, but maintained her composure. She nodded without saying a word.

"I thought so," said Mrs Acres. "You learn things, working in a hospital. Hear names and such. 'Say nothing's best', was always our motto. I was hoping you'd send somebody, *anybody*. I just didn't know what to do."

"You've told her."

The voice made Gwen jump in her chair. Looking up at the door, she saw Colin standing in the doorway, but he was different now. His face had curled up into an animalistic sneer, the upper lip parted in the centre, all the way up to his nose, which was snubbed and curled forward. His eyes were a luminous green, the pupils narrower; vertical slits that bisected each iris. When he spoke it was not in his previous plodding monotone, but with a snarl.

"Enough," said Mrs Acres firmly, "*enough*. This can't go on, Colin. Look at you... This isn't *you*. You have to listen to her."

Colin turned back to Gwen and growled softly, one paw inching closer to her face. Gwen looked into his eyes and for a moment glimpsed something childlike, hopeless and lost, in those glowing jade embers.

"You have to believe me," said Gwen. "I promise we won't hurt you."

Colin stepped back, still purring, his head hung low. Then turned suddenly and left the room, slamming the door behind him.

Bracing herself against the mantelpiece, Mrs Acres began to sob.

"It's my fault. I should have told somebody then, when all this started. It's all my fault."

Gwen crossed the room and put her arm around Mrs Acres' shoulders.

"No, no it's not," she said soothingly. "It's really not."

Taking a deep breath, Gwen found her gun and called Jack.

"Hey, Gwen!" said Jack, his usual ebullient self. "Found our monster?"

"Sort of," Gwen replied. "I'm going to need back-up. But do me a favour, Jack, come quietly; we don't need all guns blazing on this one. I'm at 37 Courtenay Road in Splott. Come as soon as you can."

"Torchwood?" Mrs Acres asked, dabbing away tears with a handkerchief.

Gwen nodded. "I'm going upstairs now, to speak to Colin. You stay here."

"No, no..." said Mrs Acres. "I don't know what he'll do, not when he's like this."

Gwen left the room, looking back at Mrs Acres just once before she closed the door. It wasn't until she was halfway up the stairs that she drew her gun again. She hadn't wanted Mrs Acres to see her doing that.

"Colin," she called as she neared the landing. Below her, in the hallway, the pendulum of the grandfather clock audibly chipped away at time, the only sound in the house other than her creaking footsteps on each stair. "Colin, I'm coming upstairs. I'm not going to hurt you."

From the bathroom she heard a loud smash, and then a moan, a low, mournful wail that seemed to pass through her like a shard of ice. She edged her way along the landing, holding the gun. The bathroom door was ajar and through it she saw the fading light of day reflecting off white tiles.

Then she saw the blood.

She nudged the door open with one foot and braced both arms, aiming the gun into the room. But there was no need. Colin lay in the bath, one arm hanging limply over its side, his throat gashed wide open, a shard of broken mirror in one hand. He wasn't yet dead, but he was bleeding profusely, and his purring was now little more than a dry rasp.

Colin looked up at Gwen with drowsy, half-closed eyes, and nodded. Then he was dead.

Jack and Ianto arrived minutes later. They took care of the body while Gwen comforted Mrs Acres. Jack had suggested they give the old woman a dose of retcon before leaving, but Gwen insisted they didn't.

"Then there won't be a funeral?" asked Mrs Acres, watching them load the anonymous black body bag into the SUV.

Gwen shook her head.

"It's like he was never here," said Mrs Acres. "Maybe it's better that way."

Gwen turned to her and saw tears welling up in her eyes once more. She held the old woman close in one last comforting embrace before Jack gestured to her from the driver's seat of the SUV.

They left Mrs Acres standing on the doorstep of her house, a scrunched up handkerchief held to her mouth. Gwen didn't take her eyes off her until they'd turned the corner onto Moorland Road.

"I feel terrible just leaving her like this."

"What else *could* you do?" said Jack. "You may have just saved her life."

"No," said Gwen. "I didn't save her life. He did." ▨

"Colin," said Mrs Acres, "I had to. It's for the best. You need help."

He snapped his head in her direction and growled. Looking down, Gwen saw his hands bunching together, the knuckles cracking and the fingernails curling into razor-sharp claws. She sprang to her feet and drew her gun.

"Please," she said, "Colin... I've got friends who might be able to help you."

"You're lying!" Colin growled, swinging at Gwen with one clawed hand, tearing the gun from her grasp and throwing it across the room.

Gwen took a step backwards and fell against the sideboard. Colin towered over her, his hands reaching out towards her throat.

"What, then, will your *friends* do with me?" he hissed. "Experiment on me, perhaps? Lock me away?"

"No," pleaded Gwen, "they *can* help you. I promise. They'll do everything they can to help you."

Colin said nothing. He leaned close to her, his mouth only inches away from her face, his jaws opening to reveal canine teeth that had become fangs, the rancid smell of rotting meat on his breath.

"Colin, stop!" said Mrs Acres, in a tone that was at once more self-assured and maternal.

Colin turned his head to look at her and grunted, his heavy breaths purring in his throat.

IT'S ALL TOO MUCH FOR ONE CAPTAIN IN THE EPISODE KISS KISS, BANG, BANG! READ OUR INTERVIEW WITH CAPTAINS JACK (**JOHN BARROWMAN**) AND JOHN (**JAMES MARSTERS**), TO GET THE LOWDOWN ON THE SPECTACULAR SERIES TWO OPENER.

O, CAPTAIN MY CAPTAIN

JULY 2007. RIHANNA IS STILL number one with the strangely appropriate Umbrella as Britain contends with severe rain and flooding. Conditions have taken their toll on Torchwood's tightly planned schedule, but cast and crew are undaunted as they prepare for their latest night shoot, 140 feet above the city, on the roof of one of Cardiff's tallest office blocks.

Fortunately, tonight proves mercifully dry and clear, and the cityscape twinkles in the darkness as John Barrowman and James Marsters block out their major scene. They are confined to one quarter of the rooftop, where a false floor has been constructed, to make the perimeter wall seem dangerously low.

"Don't look down!" laughs John, whose character, Captain Jack Harkness, will end this scene plummeting to yet another grisly death, courtesy of stuntman Curtis Rivers and a very big hydraulic crane.

"Man, I gotta get my guitar up here!" says James, who plays Jack's erstwhile partner, the villainous Captain John Hart.

With the sequence planned out, the crew continues to set up, and John and James retire to the floor below, where the (closed) Sky Café offers sofas and warmth. Both actors make time during their breaks to talk to Torchwood magazine, despite the perilously tight schedule, and John even finds the energy to amuse and entertain the crew as the clock moves ever closer to sunrise.

Indeed, the energy levels always seem to go up whenever John is around. Given the intensive night work and constant action that the show demands, it's almost as if he has residual Rift energy coursing through his veins. But in the middle of the night in the grip of a cold, wet summer, it's hard to see what there is to laugh and joke about.

"It is a lot of fun," John insists, however. "If it wasn't, I would leave. I wouldn't want anyone to think we spend our days messing about, because we do work really hard. But I always make sure I have a good time, and I do my best to make sure that everybody else does as well."

It's a responsibility he doesn't take lightly, treating the crew to bursts of song, numerous theatrical voices and, if he's feeling especially cheeky, well timed comedy flatulence. But doesn't looking out for everyone else make his days that extra bit harder?

"Well, I'm the leading man, so I do feel I have that element of responsibility. I was trained that a leading man should always

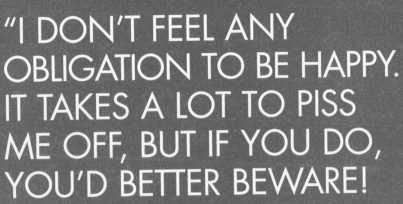

"I DON'T FEEL ANY OBLIGATION TO BE HAPPY. IT TAKES A LOT TO PISS ME OFF, BUT IF YOU DO, YOU'D BETTER BEWARE!"

look after his company. But I don't feel any obligation to go on and be happy. That's just the way I am. Eve can see if I'm not happy, and we'll have a talk about it. So we all support each other. In general it takes a lot to piss me off, but if you do, you'd better beware!"

That supportiveness must come in handy, given the long hours and frayed nerves that come with making a modern, big-budget TV show. In the months that a show like Torchwood is in production, the cast must become almost a surrogate family for each other.

"Oh, sure. We're very like a family. We kept in touch when we weren't filming at the start of last year, even if it was only over the phone. Coming back for series two was like stepping into an old pair of slippers. Everything fits perfectly and we're all very, very comfortable with each other. It wasn't hard at all."

Though the episode being filmed on the roof will be the first of the new series, it is not, in fact, the first to be made, so those reliably comfy slippers have seen several weeks of wear by now. During that time, John has had a chance to reacquaint himself with a much happier Jack than the one we saw in the first series of Torchwood. So does he prefer his character now he's found the right kind of Doctor?

"I actually enjoy both Jacks," he says, thoughtfully. "And though he is a little more easy going in this series, he still has a darker side, and I enjoy playing that.

"But that's the beauty of what I call serial television, because every week you are learning something new about the character, and you always get to play it slightly different as they grow and develop. There's still a lot we don't know about

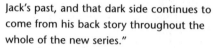

Jack's past, and that dark side continues to come from his back story throughout the whole of the new series."

With so much unexplored history in Jack's life, is it tempting to fill in the gaps that the TV show hasn't got round to yet?

"No, I leave that stuff entirely up to the writers," he says. "Unless it's something I totally disagree with – which to this day has not happened because I trust the people who are writing the scripts – I maintain that I am the actor, not the writer, and seeing what the writers do is what keeps my job exciting when I go in every day."

But without a fixed idea of what Jack's been up to these last hundred years, isn't it difficult to strike the right balance between light and shade?

"I'll be totally honest with you," he laughs, "I really don't analyse those things a lot! I treat every little scene as a little movie in itself, and if it doesn't work, the director will tell me. But nine times out of 10, it does. Part of being an actor is learning not to think. You have to remember your lines, but if you start to analyse it, you lose the whole spontaneity of the situation."

Spontaneity is clearly important on a show like Torchwood, where your understanding of a character can be turned 180 degrees by a choice line of dialogue or an unexpected twist. The whole team undergoes big changes in series two, but for the ever constant Jack, life-ending events are just as likely as life-changing ones. So is it hard to find new ways to die when you're one of the most murdered men on television?

"Yes, that takes an awful lot of effort. You can't make too big a thing out of it every time: if you're stabbed, you bleed, you look at the people, you go down, you die. But the one thing that we need to

show is the pain and distress that Jack goes through when he's coming back to life. So we have established a way in which Jack returns from the dead, which is always with an extreme gasp of air and with panic in his face.

"It could very easily become something that you take for granted, so this year we've made sure to crank up the jeopardy that's involved, and to show that Gwen and the others never know if this could be the time that he's not coming back. When he does come around, Gwen also tries to be there to calm him, because she understands what it is that he's going through."

There will be no Gwen around to pick Jack up tonight, however, when he faces some especially cranked-up jeopardy at the hands of Captain John and a rapidly approaching pavement. As the star of the show, John isn't allowed to do

the falling stunt himself, but he and James Marsters will film the preceding sequence dangerously close to the rooftop edge (dangerous looking, at least: both actors are wearing safety harnesses). It's something that requires a lot of trust from two men who barely know each other, so presumably the pair of them hit it off okay?

"Oh yeah, James is great!" confirms John. "The first day we worked together, we had to beat each other up and have a full-on snog! James had never done that with a guy before, but he totally went for it. He was a bit nervous at first, but I said, 'It's just a kiss! I'm not gonna shove my tongue down your throat!'

"I'm ashamed to admit I never watched Buffy," he continues. "So I didn't have any preconceived image of James, though I did know his character, Spike. You can't have been on this planet for the last 10 years and

FIGHTING TALK

CAST AND CREW PULL NO PUNCHES REGARDING THAT KISS, AND A VERY MEMORABLE BARROOM BRAWL…

CHRIS CHIBNALL (WRITER): "We talked a lot about the fight sequence being sexy, rather than brutal. It's a kind of foreplay, so you shouldn't be hiding your face from the blood and gore. In the script, I said it should be like Women In Love, where they wrestle naked in front of the fire – but without the fire or the nudity! So they read that, and dressed the set with roaring fires on the screens in the bar, bless them! I think it's brilliant!"

ASHLEY WAY (DIRECTOR): "The brief was for an epic encounter, and I was adamant that we should use John and James wherever we could, to make it as real as possible. I defy anyone to tell when it's not them, without using the pause button. We mapped it out a few days beforehand with the stunt guys, and it took us the best part of a day to shoot, so it was a big number. And when you're in a tight TV schedule, taking a whole day out to film a one-minute bar fight is really quite significant. I think it sums up the whole episode really, because it's sexy, brutal and fun, and it's got a kind of swagger to it."

TOM LUCY (STUNT COORDINATOR): "The asks for the fight were quite major. Ashley wanted it to have elements of martial arts, but also to be rough and ready: a mixture of all different fights. So we blocked it out

on site using stunt doubles, and showed the actors, to work out what was best for both of us. Because, obviously, I might throw the best left-hand in the world, but if the actor doesn't, then you've got a major problem.

"We didn't have to change too much, though, and when we actually did the shoot, the ratio of actors to stuntmen was probably as high as 80%. It's determined by ability, and sometimes my job is to protect the actors from themselves. But James and John were just fantastic, and you can really see it's them – not stuntmen trying to cover their faces with their moves. Everyone was really pleased, and I got a lot of pride out of that."

JOHN BARROWMAN: "The fight scene is my favourite moment in episode one, because we did practically all the stunts ourselves. They filmed a lot more than they could use, so maybe it will turn up an a DVD one day!"

JAMES MARSTERS: "The drinking was the hardest part of that scene! It's very hard to chug a whole bottle of liquid, so when you see it in movies they always cut away. But I found a way to do it, and I had to do it 13 times! I drank 13 litres of water in an hour and a half. So we'd do a take, and I'd drink a bottle, go to the bathroom, barf it up, come back out, and do it all over again. Ugh!"

CHRIS CHIBNALL: "The kiss! How could they not? I just knew that the first moment they met would have to be a kiss followed by a punch. It was so clear to me, there was just no other way to do it. There must be a whole universe of Jack and John stories to be told, and I would happily write them!"

JAMES MARSTERS: "John was so professional about the kiss that I got relaxed really fast. I think he saw I was a little nervous at first, but afterwards I felt embarrassed that I'd ever been shy about it! John's a good leader, and approaches things like an actor should. He finds out everyone's comfort level, and keeps everyone feeling safe all the time."

JOHN BARROWMAN: "I knew James hadn't kissed a guy before, so I told him the best thing was just to go for it. If you anaylse it, you just get nervous and freaked out. So we had some gum and rinsed our mouths, and then we just kissed. I think his girlfriend thought it was quite horny, actually!"

"I'M AN OPENLY GAY MAN PLAYING AN OMNISEXUAL HERO, WHO IS LOVED ON BOTH SIDES OF THE ATLANTIC! HOW COULD I NOT BE PROUD OF THAT?"

So, with the show breaking new ground, geographically and sexually, does John have any other ambitions for Captain Jack?

"I'd like Jack to have a boat!" he laughs, setting his sights less loftily. "Also, I'd love to do a show about Torchwood Two, where we meet the funny little guy who runs it!"

This other outpost of the organisation, mentioned briefly at the start of the first series, is based in Glasgow, where John was born, and from where he still draws a strong Scottish accent, as required.

"I've always said to Russell that if we do that story, I'd really like to play the Scottish guy!" he says, Scottishly. "Or we could get David Tennant to do it, wearing makeup so you couldn't tell it was him! Sometimes I talk to David in my Scottish accent and it totally freaks him out!"

It sounds like a surefire hit for series three, but for now John is sufficiently enthused about series two not to get too attached to the idea – or the voice. Besides, rehearsals beckon once again, and the world isn't ready for a Scottish Captain Jack just yet.

"I just think this is a spectacular episode to start the series," he says, adopting his more usual tone as we part. "We're not walking anymore: we're running. We know where we're going, and this episode is going to launch the rest of the series like an aircraft carrier. We'll be firing at you so fast you won't know what's hit you!" T

Turn the page for more on episode one, from guest star James Marsters!

not know who Spike is and what he was! But when he came on set he wasn't Spike from Buffy, he was James in Torchwood. So, though we knew where he was coming from, we welcomed him like any new cast member, and it was really good."

With the Buffy star's appearance in the new series, Torchwood should see its burgeoning US fanbase grow bigger than ever. But just two weeks before James found himself on a rooftop in Cardiff, John was already fielding questions about the show at BBC America's launch event for series one, in the slightly more glamourous surrounds of LA. Later that year, it would go on to break all the channel's viewing records, but how was Torchwood received at that first transatlantic event?

"The welcome we got in the States was incredible!" enthuses John. "We were nervous about taking the show Stateside, just as we were nervous when we launched in the UK. But we were a success here, and they just love us over there! We thought the

US audience might have a problem with some of the sexuality, but in fact it's like a breath of fresh air for them, and so they welcomed us with open arms."

Getting mainstream acceptance for a character like Jack is no mean feat in the US, so does John take pride in breaking down some of those barriers?

"Of course I do!" he exclaims. "We're part of history! I'm an openly gay man playing an omnisexual hero, who is loved by men, women and children on both sides of the Atlantic! How could I not be proud of that?

"Plus, we get to expand upon it even more this year, because we are following through on things that were mentioned in series one. In the first episode, Jack asks Ianto out on a date, so you'll just have to wait and see where that goes! I think it's great to see that the leading man doesn't always have to fall for the leading lady. A lot of the comments I get, from female fans especially, say that they want to see Ianto and Jack get it on!"

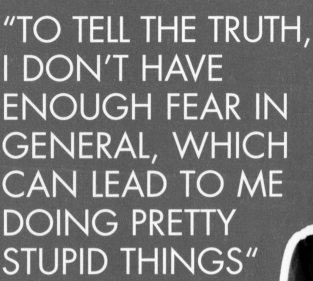

"TO TELL THE TRUTH, I DON'T HAVE ENOUGH FEAR IN GENERAL, WHICH CAN LEAD TO ME DOING PRETTY STUPID THINGS"

AS SOMEONE BEST KNOWN for playing a creature of the night, it seems appropriate that James Marsters should be talking to Torchwood magazine sometime after the witching hour. But, with dark hair and a US accent, the actor and singer is nothing like his most famous creation, Spike from Buffy the Vampire Slayer. And, despite our late meeting, he is wide awake and full of enthusiasm for his work and his surroundings.

"I love Cardiff," he says, surveying the scene from the 11th floor Sky Café. "It reminds me of Seattle, which is my favourite town. I think art is infused into the culture here, so I don't feel like the freaky carny. Maybe everyone's a freaky carny here, which is great.

"Luckily I don't have a problem with heights," he adds. "To tell you the truth, I don't have enough fear in general, which can lead to me doing pretty stupid things. When I was 20, me and a friend decided to shimmy down a 900-foot rock fissure in Yosemite, without ropes or anything. We got screwed, but inch by inch we made our way out, so this isn't too bad compared to that."

Resplendent in red and military braid, James cuts a very distinctive dash in his Torchwood outfit, but that's not all he could cut with the impressive sword that has been at his side for most of the night.

"The sword never comes out," he insists. "It's a beautiful, snakeskin Samurai sword, but it hasn't been dulled or bated, so it does not want to come out of there. It's not razor sharp, but it's sharp enough to cause a problem if you were to start having 'fun' with it. I only unsheathed it during

MAKING AN ENTRANCE

THE STORY BEHIND THE DRAMATIC VISUAL EFFECTS THAT HERALD TORCHWOOD'S RETURN TO TV...

the photoshoot, and I was very careful. If you gave me a dulled sword, then I'd show you some moves!"

James' familiarity with swordplay comes from his time on stage, though he's yet to wield a blade on screen. "If you do Shakespeare, then you learn swords," he explains. "In the theatre, you don't get a stuntman – and you learn how to die, downstage, and not breathe. That's the hard part! One time on Buffy I also did some quarterstaff work, and that stuff is really hard. Darth Maul rocks!"

Surprisingly, it's been nearly five years since the end of Buffy, and in that time James has gone on to make well received appearances in shows such as Angel and Smallville. Now, with his guest turn in the series premiere of Torchwood, it looks as if he's trying to corner the market in grown-up, intelligent sci-fi on both sides of the Atlantic.

"It's true!" he admits. "I wanted to produce a prequel series of Star Trek a few years back, but Enterprise got there first! Then I came over here on tour, and I got to see Doctor Who, because one of my tour managers was obsessed with it.

"It was a fabulous plot, equivalent to three or four episodes of American TV, and that's when I knew I wanted to work on a Russell T Davies production! So I called my agent, and here I am. They said it was amazing synchronicity, because they didn't know who to cast for this character before I got in touch."

It's not hard to see why Torchwood's producers had a hard time thinking of a suitable candidate for Captain John. Every inch a match for Captain Jack, but without the compassion and friendship that comes

"In the first draft of the script, Captain John came through the Rift on a surfboard," says Chris Chibnall, Torchwood's lead writer and the man behind Kiss Kiss, Bang Bang.

"It was meant to follow on from the 'pandimensional surfboard' [in the Doctor Who episode Boom Town], but we decided it would look cooler if John just calmly walked out of the Rift, as if it was the sort of thing he might do every day."

The decision made life a little easier for The Mill, the company responsible for visual effects in both Torchwood and Doctor Who, but it still left the question of precisely what the Rift itself should look like.

"We'd seen the Rift before, in Boom Town and in series one of Torchwood," says Marie Jones from The Mill. "But do all manifestations of the Rift look the same? When we sat down with the rest of the team, we decided that the answer was no, and for this series it should be something warmer and more magical. So we went for a mix of orange and gold particles, and everyone seemed to like it. I hope they still do, as it comes up again throughout the series!"

The Mill also provided the various hologram effects seen in episode one, treating footage shot on green screen, and compositing it into various scenes.

"We had to create three holograms," says Marie. "And we tried to give them all a different look, because each one comes from a different source. There's Captain Jack's wrist projection, which had to match the blue hologram we'd seen him use in Doctor Who; then there's Captain John's equivalent of the same thing, which was specified in the script as being more flash-looking and full colour. Lastly, there's the image that comes from the artefact itself, which we gave a sort of golden look, based on the actual prop.

"We also painted in a lot more containers for the scenes at the docks, to make it seem like a much bigger space, but you shouldn't even register that that is an effect. Sometimes it's the things the audience doesn't notice that we're most proud of at The Mill!"

"EVE IS AMAZING BECAUSE SHE CARES SO MUCH. EVERY TIME I ASK IF I'M GETTING TOO PHYSICAL, SHE SAYS, 'NO, MAN! TRY TO HURT ME! YOU CAN'T DO IT!'"

from being part of a team, John needed to be dynamic and sexy, yet utterly hard and ruthless: a dark mirror on Jack's past.

"He is what Jack used to be," James explains. "Though I have a feeling that Jack was even meaner and nastier, if that's possible. I think it's my job to make that old life seem as seductive as I can, so it's a question of which path Jack will choose. He's just come back, and his team are mad at him. So is he going to be a responsible leader, or is he going to screw it up? Captain John has essentially come back for the lover that left him, so there's a lot of darkness happening there.

"In a lot of ways, this role is very much like Spike was in my first three episodes of Buffy," he continues. "After those three episodes, Spike was always taken down a peg, because Joss [Whedon, Buffy creator] didn't want the audience thinking he was cool. They basically deconstructed him, but it had the opposite effect, and he became cooler than ever: the outsider's outsider, in a show of outsiders! But the role of Captain John is about unrepentant evil, and having as much fun with it as possible. I just wish Spike had been like that a little longer, to be honest."

It's clear James relishes the opportunity to be bad, but isn't there a part of him that would like to play the heroic lead every now and again?

"Well, I'm kind of a method actor, so I put myself through real hell with this stuff!" he laughs. "I still get cool roles, it's just that I keep playing guys who lose! If you play a lead, the difference is that you have to function as a template for every audience member to relate to, so it can be constricting. I did it on stage more, and you find that you can't make that many specific choices. There's a definite art to it, but with villains, you can throw in far more of the weirdness of your own character, and make a very specific person. Everybody has a nasty person inside of them, and that's where I've had to go with this."

As a way to exorcise one's demons, that attitude certainly beats some of Captain John's own methods, but it also sounds like a lot of hard work. So has Torchwood been a good experience for James?

"Oh, it's just been brilliant," he says. "I got relaxed really fast, because everyone is so professional. John is such a good leader, and Eve is just amazing! They're

RED ALERT

CAPTAIN JOHN IS DRESSED TO KILL...

"It's all about the costume, isn't it?" says James Marsters on the subject of his distinctive threads. "When I saw it for the first time, I thought, 'Now, this is gonna be good!'"

Like all the outfits on Torchwood, the military jacket and jeans combo is the work of costume designer, Ray Holman. "It's based on real military stuff," he says. "But it's nothing like any real regiment. Russell T Davies had suggested a grenadier's coat, but when I went to look at them, they were all much too long, and [executive producer] Julie Gardner was determined to see some bum action!

"So I found a few examples of shorter mess jackets, which are much plainer, and one which I really liked the braid on, and we made something up that combined the two looks.

"The next thing we did was work out where all the weapons were going to be. I didn't get to fit James until the day before he was on set, so I worked it all out on myself with some help from the art department. The belts and the holsters and the sword took some thinking about, but by the time we presented it to James it was all sorted, really."

all wonderful actors, who want to have fun in real life, so they know you have to learn your lines and know your game if you want to avoid a lot of unnecessary drama. And I am used to a lot of unnecessary drama. Not on Smallville, not on Angel, and not here, but on other shows, and it really saps your energy.

"But with someone like Eve, it's just amazing, because she cares so much," he enthuses. "We were handcuffed together yesterday, and I had to swallow the key. It wasn't written, but instinctively she just grabbed my throat to stop me swallowing it! That's brilliant. And every time I ask if I'm getting too physical, she says, 'No, man! Hit me harder! Try to hurt me! You can't do it!' It's so much fun when everyone is like that."

The camaraderie doesn't end when the cameras go off, either. In between filming for Torchwood, James took the opportunity to play a live gig at popular Cardiff venue The Point, where he invited fellow musician Gareth David Lloyd (Ianto) to perform with him on stage.

"Oh, that was the high point of the evening!" says James. "He was so good and he really rocked out! Now my girlfriend's

singing his song all day! And Cardiff is such a great audience. I had the best show of my life in Newport a few years ago, when I was with my band Ghost of the Robot. In other parts of the world, I think the audience tries to pretend you're a movie, but in Wales, there's a sense that we're all together in the same room, and we can really make something happen. When you get that, it's just gold."

James' guitar also travels with him on set, and comes out several times between takes for impromptu song-writing sessions. So was he never tempted to pursue music as his primary career?

"No, I made that choice when I was at college," he says. "I was playing music in bars and doing a lot of plays, and I made the decision to focus on acting. But my guitar remains my safety net, and it comes out so much here because Cardiff is just so wonderful for songwriting. I've written two full songs while I've been here, and I've got two more that I'm working on. They almost come out too fast to write."

So what is it about acting that won out over music? And why does he need it as a safety net?

> "MUSIC IS LIKE ALGEBRA. YOU GET THE SAME CONNECTION WHEN SOMETHING IS LEARNED OR UNDERSTOOD, AND THAT'S A VERY POWERFUL MOMENT."

"I just enjoy being part of a group that is functioning harmoniously," he says. "Music can have that, but there's a lot of alone time, too. And, frankly, when I got into acting, it was to find a sense of community and harmony that I couldn't have at home.

"But now, being on set for 12 hours a day, things can start to bother you," he admits. "And that's where music comes in. If I play my guitar, I feel less tired, I can remember my lines better, and I can deal with whatever frustrations might come along. For me, music is like algebra. You don't have to know math to understand the formula, but you get the same physiological connection in the brain when something is learned or understood, and that's a very powerful moment."

So, having had such a good time on the set of Torchwood, could there be a musical collaboration with that other popular artiste, John Barrowman, in the offing?

"Ha! I really don't know if he has the time," Marsters laughs. "He was out doing another television show over the weekend, and there's some other show he's trying to close the deal on. He's a machine! But if I could get him for an afternoon? Then yeah," he grins. "I think that would be really cool." ⊺

MARSTERS AT WORK

FROM CAMERAMAN TO CAPTAIN JOHN, JAMES MARSTERS' LIFE ON FILM...

TELEVISION

Torchwood (2008) Captain John Hart
Chasing The Devil (2008) Ted Bundy
Smallville (2005-2008) Professor Milton Fine/Brainiac
Without A Trace (2007) Grant Mars
Saving Grace (2007) Dudley Payne
Cool Money (2005) Bobby Comfort
The Mountain (2004) Ted Tunney
Angel (1999-2004) Spike
Spider-Man (2003) Sergei (voice)
Andromeda (2001) Charlemagne Bolivar
The Enforcers (2001) Sullivan McManus
Strange Frequency 2 (2001) Mitch Brand
Strange Frequency (2001) Mitch Brand
Winding Roads (1999) Billy Johnson
Millennium (1999) Eric Swan
Buffy the Vampire Slayer (1997-2003) Spike
Moloney (1997) Billy O'Hara
Medicine Ball (1995) Mickey Collins
Northern Exposure (1992-1993) Bellhop/Reverend Harding

FILM

Dragonball (2008) Piccolo
PS I Love You (2007) John McCarthy
Superman: Doomsday (2007) Lex Luthor (voice)
Shadow Puppets (2007) Jack
Chance (2002) Simon
House On Haunted Hill (1999) Channel 3 Cameraman

The Beauty Of Our Weapons

By Andy Lane

"**W**"e've got a problem," Ianto said as he rushed into the Hub.

"Narrow it down for us," Owen murmured without looking up from his medical computer screen. "Is it a coffee-related emergency? Water not at precisely the right temperature? Run out of Jamaican Blue Mountain coffee beans perhaps? Or perhaps it's something to do with that little cubby hole you sit in waiting for visitors who never arrive. Wallpaper started peeling, has it?"

Ignoring Owen's needling, Ianto moved across to the doorway of Jack's office. He was brandishing a yellowed sheet of paper. "There's something missing from the archives!"

"How do you know?" Toshiko called from her workbench, where she was soldering an alien circuit board that looked more like a jewelled spider's web than anything functional.

Captain Jack Harkness moved out from the shadows behind his desk and walked across to the doorway. Ianto stood there, letting Jack invade his personal space for a moment, before moving back a step.

"Because he's been conducting a cross-check of the files with what we've actually got in the storerooms." Jack replied. "Part of an audit that we do every few years." His eyes locked with Ianto's. "Are you sure it's missing? Could it have been misfiled, put in the wrong place?"

Ianto shook his head. "Too big. I've checked everywhere. There's no sign of it."

"Too *big*? What do the files say it is?" Jack asked.

Ianto consulted the sheet of paper in his hand. "The description here says it's an alien artefact, spherical, about two metres in diameter, found near Ystrad Mynach in 1938 after drifting through the Rift. Possibly a work of art — a sculpture of some kind." He frowned at the paper. "I think this is your writing, boss."

Jack took the sheet of paper and glanced at it. "Could be," he said. "I can't say I remember writing it, though. Then again, there're several marriage certificates and a declaration of war out there that I could say the same about." He frowned. "A work of art? Can't say we get many of those coming through. Weapons, yes. Creatures with teeth and an attitude, definitely. But works of art?"

Gwen was coming down the stairs from where she had been sitting in the conference room, reading a file. "You must be able to remember putting a two-metre sculpture into storage," she said.

Jack shrugged. "If it doesn't try to kill me or make love to me, I tend to put it out of my mind." He thought for a moment. "We need to find it."

"Why?" Owen questioned, looking up from his screen. "It's not dangerous. It's probably the alien equivalent of that crap painting of dogs sitting round a table playing poker. We've got more important things to worry about."

"Not the point," Jack said, his voice echoing around the Hub in a way that nobody else in the team had ever managed. "If we start letting stuff out of the archives, where will it stop? Ever heard of the Cargo Cults in the South Seas? They were primitive tribes who were living in splendid isolation until they saw aircraft flying over their islands. They built up a big religion based around these aircraft, perverting their own culture into something unnatural." He paused, frowning. "They ended up worshipping the Duke of Edinburgh, for reasons I never really understood. Anyway, we have a responsibility to keep Earth's culture from becoming contaminated."

"Earth for Earthlings?" Gwen challenged from the steps. "Isn't that a bit racist?"

"Well, species-ist — technically," put in Tosh.

"You can have alien art when you're ready for it," Jack replied levelly. "In the meantime, you and Tosh see if you can work out where the sculpture went. Ianto: you and I will come up with a theory about how someone could sneak a two-metre diameter sphere out of this place without being noticed."

"What about me?" Owen asked, aggrieved.

"You can take over Ianto's work on that cross-check. I want to know what else is missing. And put a fresh pot of coffee on; we're going to need it."

"The obvious starting point," Tosh said to Gwen later as they both sat at her workbench, "is to do a Web search. I've developed a search engine that not only scans the entire Web, but also piggybacks on WiFi and Bluetooth links to hack into private databases, industrial servers and Government computers, and report back."

"Sneaky," Gwen said. "It's a good thing we can be trusted not to abuse this kind of technology, isn't it?"

"Actually," Tosh admitted, blushing, "I did once use it to check up on a girl Owen was seeing. She was a gold-digger — trying to get him to buy her jewellery and designer clothes. I wanted to prove to him that she was no good."

"What happened?"

"Before I could tell him, he somehow persuaded her to pay for first class plane tickets to St Lucia, then he dumped her after a few days and had an affair with an air hostess." She shook her head. "He's incorrigible."

"That's one word for it," Gwen said dryly.

Tosh's screen showed what appeared to Gwen to be a typical search engine page, but with the Torchwood logo hovering above it. Tosh typed in a description of the missing sculpture, then pressed 'Return'. For a few moments, nothing happened, and then a short list of search results flashed up on the screen.

"Most of these we can discount," Tosh said, scanning down through the results. "They name an artist, or date the sculpture to a time before we know it was discovered and put into the Torchwood archives. But one or two of them... Look at this! It's a newspaper article about the private collection of a rich Welsh philanthropist named Ashley ab Hugh who had a passion for non-representational art. The centrepiece of his collection was a large sphere that appeared to be lit from within, and had shapes drifting across the surface."

"Sounds like our target," Gwen said. "Does it say what happened to it?"

Tosh shook her head. "There's just the one reference. After that, the trail runs cold. We're out of luck."

"Not so fast," Gwen replied. "When technology fails we can always fall back on time-honoured investigative methods. Let's go and take a look for ourselves."

Ianto stood in the shadows and darkness of the Torchwood archives, listening to the *drip drip drip* of water falling from the brick ceiling and the *beep beep beep* of the scanner that Captain Jack was holding.

"There're traces all around here," Jack said. "Whatever that sculpture is, it was giving off radiation."

"Harmful?" Ianto asked as casually as he could. "Anything that would hamper my chances of having kids?"

Jack glanced over at him. "I think radiation is the least of your concerns in that area," he said. "But none the less, the radiation is only slightly above background levels. Extrapolating backwards as best I can without Tosh being here, I reckon even that when it was discovered it was probably barely more than slightly warm and tingly."

"Tingly?"

"That's a scientific term. Probably part of the artistic effect."

Ianto raised an eyebrow.

Jack looked around. "And although it won't tell us where the sculpture is now, the radiation might tell us the path it took out of here..."

pedestals. The paintings were blobs of colour with no identifiable features, and the sculptures looked like they were either half-melted or half-grown.

"Would you like a tour?" Williams said.

"Actually," Gwen replied, "we're looking for a particular piece. A large globe, about the size of a person, looking like it's lit from within. Shapes on the surface that appear to move. Ring any bells?"

"Ah." Williams shook his head sadly. "'The cursed statue'. If I had three pounds fifty for everyone who has asked me about that..."

"Cursed?" Toshiko bristled scientifically.

"Mr ab Hugh collected numerous non-representational works of art throughout his life. That sculpture was the last thing Mr ab Hugh bought. Apparently he found it in an auction of rare and unusual items. There was something about it that fascinated him. He would sit and watch it for hours, not moving, not eating. And that's where they found him, in the end. Sitting in front of it. Stark staring mad."

"When was this?" Tosh breathed.

"The thirteenth of August, 1963."

Gwen couldn't help herself. "How did they know he was mad?"

"Because he was tearing thin strips of flesh off his face and decorating the surface of the sculpture with them."

"Okay. That's fairly convincing. What happened to him?"

"He died of septicemia three weeks later, screaming about the colours he could see. The bright, bright colours."

"And the sculpture?" Gwen had a bad feeling about this, but she had to ask. "What happened to it? Is it on display somewhere in here, or has it been locked away for posterity?"

Williams shook his head sadly. "The executors of Mr ab Hugh's will were concerned about the notoriety of the piece. They sold it."

"To whom?"

"An anonymous buyer."

"Of course they did." Gwen shook her head. "I should have known it wouldn't have been that easy." I don't suppose you have any clues about who this anonymous buyer was?"

Williams thought for a moment. "I remember someone else came looking for the sculpture, back in the 1970s. He was a private investigator. He wanted a receipt for the entry fee, which is why I remembered his name, and that's why I noticed in the paper three days later that he had been found dead. It was in the docks area. He'd been shot. There was a police investigation, but they never found his killer. I think they put it down to gangs and drugs. That's all I have. Sorry."

Gwen turned to go, but Tosh stayed facing Williams. "Did you ever see the sculpture yourself?" she asked.

"Once," he admitted. He raised his left hand and gazed at it. The skin on the back was corrugated and purple with old scar tissue, as if he had tried to pluck it off with his fingernails, many years ago. "Only once. But I still remember the light, and the shapes. I still remember them."

The massive 1930s house was all white plaster and red brick. It was set back from the road, isolated from the well-to-do Cardiff suburb where it sat by a driveway, metal fences and security cameras. A sign by the road identified it as the Ashley ab Hugh Museum, entrance fee £3.50, open Tuesdays and Thursdays from 10.00 until 16.00.

"Got any cash?" Gwen asked Toshiko as they entered the front hall.

"It's an optional payment," wheezed the man who sat behind a cash desk just inside the front door. His sparse hair was wispy and white, and his suit had seen better days. The name badge on his larger-than-fashionable lapels said: 'Bill Williams'.

"Then why doesn't it say that on the sign?"

Williams frowned. "Because people wouldn't pay it if we told them it was optional."

"Then why did you tell *us*?" Tosh asked.

"Because if I hadn't you might not have come in, and we haven't had any visitors here for months. We're a bit off the beaten track. Not in any of the guidebooks, you see. No 'website'." He pronounced the word with distaste.

Gwen looked around. The hall was painted white, brightly lit, and full of paintings hanging on the walls and small sculptures on

---

The trail of radioactivity led Jack and Ianto towards the Hub and then off to one side, to one of the massive arched tunnels that led away from their base and towards God knew where.

"You'd think there would be a map of these things," Ianto complained, staring into the darkness.

"I walked along one, once," Jack said. "For four days. It just kept going straight, no turns or twists, aiming somewhere to the north-east. I did work out that it was heading towards Glasgow, but I didn't have enough sandwiches to check if it went all the way. Not that it would

have stopped me, if it had been important, but dying of hunger repeatedly for several weeks wouldn't have done much for my manly physique."

"You could have used a motorbike," Ianto pointed out. "It's faster."

"What, wear all that leather and pose astride a throbbing engine with nobody to see me? If I'm going to ride a motorbike I'll do it in public, thank you." He sighed, and shook his head. "If you ask me, and you probably will at some stage, that sculpture was sneaked out and sold by someone in the Torchwood team back in the 1950s. We had some rotten apples in the barrel in those days, and there were secret auctions going on in Cardiff where collectors could buy stuff that had drifted through the Rift."

"What stopped the auctions?" Ianto asked.

"I did. I flooded the auctions — with fakes. Once people realised they weren't buying real alien stuff, the bottom dropped out of the market."

Something *beep*ed in Jack's jacket. He pulled out a small communicator and plugged it in his ear. "It's Tosh," he said after a few seconds. "They've found something."

It was dusk when Tosh and Gwen arrived at the warehouse area of the old docks. The skeletons of rusted cranes loomed over them, and the setting sun cast long shadows across the concrete wharfs and quays. Weeds and lone tufts of grass poked their way furtively through cracks, apparently hoping they wouldn't be noticed if they kept their heads down..

"This is where the body was discovered," Gwen said. "The police files had a sketch map. I doubt this place has changed much since then."

"What are we looking for?" Tosh asked, glancing around nervously. "I mean, there wouldn't be any evidence still here; not after all that time."

"According to the file, the police searched the local area, but there was one warehouse they couldn't get into. It was padlocked, they couldn't trace the owner, and they didn't have enough evidence to get a warrant to force it open. So they left it."

"So?"

"So we know something they didn't, which is that the private investigator was searching for something bulky that presumably had to be stored somewhere. A warehouse seems as good a place as any. Perhaps it was bought by some collector who was keeping things in the hope they would appreciate in value in the future." She pointed to one of the corrugated metal buildings. "And that's the one."

The warehouse was still locked, apparently from the inside. It took them ten minutes and the careful application of a magnetic beam generator of alien origin to slide the bolts back on the inside of the door and push it open against rusted hinges.

The smell from inside was old and dry and dusty. Horizontal shafts of red-tinged sunlight penetrated holes in the metal walls and illuminated the cavernous interior like hundreds of coloured spotlights.

"Good God," Gwen breathed as she looked around. "If the police had got in here the file would have been a lot bigger."

The central area of the warehouse was taken up with a massive and apparently real temple, constructed from pillars and a low roof. Tapestries showing woven figures covered in blood hid the temple's interior, but did not hide the less bloody, more mummified bodies that littered the steps around its base.

Gwen and Toshiko moved closer. The bodies were sprawled in disarray; grey, papery skin covering their skeletons and cobwebs filling their eye sockets and gaping mouths. They appeared to be wearing robes covered in cabbalistic symbols embroidered in gold thread, although the colours of the material had bleached out in the heat of the summer sun and the cold of the winter.

"We're only looking for a piece of art," Gwen complained, grimacing at the nauseating sight. "Not loonies who peel their faces off. Not members of some bizarre religious cult who appear to have all died at the same time. Just a piece of art. Is that too much to ask?"

"Cult?" Toshiko asked in a small voice.

"Look at them. Hidden temple. Robes. Postures that make it appear like they've all taken poison and died in agony. It just shouts 'Jonestown' and 'the Reverend Jim Jones' at you."

"Does it?" Toshiko knelt by one of the desiccated bodies and ran a handheld sensor over the skull and the robes. "I'll send this back to the Hub. Jack and Owen can analyse the results for us."

"At the moment," Gwen said, "I'm more interested in what's behind those tapestries, inside the temple. My heart wants it to be the sculpture that these guys presumably bought off the executors of Ashley ab Hugh's estate, but my head is telling me that there's nothing there but empty space." She climbed up the steps to the temple and pulled one of the tapestries to one side. "And the score so far: head: one, heart: nil. It's looking bad for the heart."

"No sculpture?"

"Just a patch of flooring slightly less dusty than the rest, as if something had been resting there but was taken away. There are some scratch marks where I think it was dragged off, and the steps on the far side look scuffed, as if something heavy went that way."

While Toshiko took more readings of the bodies, Gwen investigated the shadowy interior of the temple. The faint ghost of incense teased her nostrils.

When she emerged, Toshiko was talking to herself. Or, rather, to someone back at the Hub.

"Owen says that there are traces of some alkaloid-based toxin on the lips and fingers of the bodies," she said, "and Jack says that the symbols on the robes are consistent with a small cult of religious fanatics that sprang up in Cardiff in the 1970s worshipping alien technology. He said, 'think Cargo Cults'."

"There's no trace of where the sculpture went," Gwen said, dispiritedly. "Assuming it was even here in the first place. I'm guessing that the cultists somehow found out about the alien sculpture and purchased it so they could really go to town on the worship front. What happened then? Did they go mad looking at it, like Ashley ab Hugh, or was it stolen from them while they were out, leaving them so ashamed that they killed themselves?"

"What about the private investigator?" Toshiko asked. "He was shot, not poisoned."

"Perhaps he stumbled upon the temple," Gwen speculated.

Tosh looked around. "I don't see any guns. And a religious cult worshipping alien technology seems more likely to use some kind of alien weapon to kill an intruder. Or a sharp blade. Just not a gun."

"You're right." Gwen considered for a moment. "I think we need to find out more about that private investigator. It's possible that he wasn't looking for the sculpture when he was killed. It's possible that he had found it, and was killed by whoever had hired him."

"Whatever happened," Toshiko said, "if I actually believed in luck rather than the random application of probability theory then I would say that sculpture was definitely bad luck for whoever came near it."

Jack and Ianto were hunched together over a computer screen when Owen walked back into the Hub. He was tired, he was dusty, and his eyes were scratchy from trying to make out scribbled notes in old files.

"I think," he announced to nobody in particular, "that there're another five items which we're supposed to have but don't. There're also three items we have but which don't appear in the records, so I guess it kind of evens itself out in the end."

Neither Jack nor Ianto reacted.

"Gwen," Jack said, "I've checked the bank statements of the private investigator on-line. His last big payment was from Dimitri Arkanovitch. He's a Russian billionaire — owns the Arkanovitch Hotel in Cardiff City Centre."

Owen looked around, but there was no sign of Gwen. Or Toshiko.

"I remember him from when I was in the police," Gwen's voice said tinnily. It took Owen a moment to realize that she was talking on a communications link. "He's tied in to the Russian Mafia."

"He probably used his criminal contacts to steal the sculpture from the cultists, and left the PI dead to stop anything leading back to him."

"Then let's pay him a visit," Gwen said. Even on the communications link, her voice sounded grim.

The Arkanovitch Hotel was triangular and hollow, built around a central atrium, with the rooms all opening onto balconies that looked out at a ceiling of green glass and a penthouse above, and a sculpted area of fountains, a small bar and restaurant seating areas below.

And in the centre of the atrium Gwen and Toshiko found the sculpture.

It was incredible. And beautiful. And stunning. Gwen's breath caught in her throat just looking at it.

There was nothing particularly complex or artistic about the sculpture. As the various clues they had been following had indicated, it was just a large sphere of some white, glassy material lit from within, sitting on a conical pedestal of what looked like black stone. At first sight it looked quite boring. But then you looked more closely at the sphere, and you saw... things. Subtle colours rippling inside, like an *aurora borealis* that had been captured and imprisoned forever. Flickering flames of cold light that seemed to move with purpose, with meaning.

When she was a child, Gwen had spent hours in front of her parents' fireplace, staring at the coals as they burned. The fire had always seemed to her to be a magical thing, and looking into the centre of the sphere, captured by its radiant beauty, she felt a connection back with the child she had once been, and could never be again.

"This isn't a sculpture," Toshiko said.

Gwen looked around. Toshiko was on her hands and knees, examining the black pedestal.

"What do you mean, it isn't a sculpture?"

"I mean..." Toshiko ran her magnetic lock-picker across the black surface. A triangular section fell into her hands. In the hollow interior, Gwen could see wiring, circuit boards, metal cylinders. All alien, but all obviously technical.

"Isn't that just the stuff that makes it light up?" Gwen asked.

"No," Jack said from behind her. "That's the stuff that makes it *blow* up."

Gwen turned. Jack, Owen and Ianto had just arrived in the hotel atrium.

"Blow up? What are you talking about?"

Toshiko glanced up at Gwen from her position on the floor. "If I understand these circuits correctly, that globe is an anti-matter explosion, caught a femto-second after detonation in a complex combination of a time field and a magnetic field. It's literally frozen in time."

"Can't you defuse it?" Gwen asked, hearing the shrillness of her voice and not liking the sound.

"It's too *late* to defuse it." Toshiko had the same tone in her voice.

"It's already gone off — only the power source is holding it back from exploding!"

From behind her, Gwen heard Ianto's voice. "What idiot exhibits a nuclear explosion as a work of art?"

"Someone who wants to smuggle a weapon into the capital city of their enemy," Jack growled. "Who could resist exhibiting a work of art, especially from someone whose planet they've conquered? It's a Trojan Horse. A booby trap; impossible to defuse and probably set off by remote control whenever its builders feel like it."

"And we're the boobies," Owen muttered.

"I think it drifted here by accident," Jack said. "It's not meant for us."

"Which will be little consolation when it goes off," Gwen pointed out.

Toshiko rummaged around inside the pedestal. Gwen could hear Jack's breath hissing through his teeth.

"Do you want the good news or the bad news?" Toshiko said, after a pause that felt like centuries.

"Does the bad news end in 'bang'?" Owen asked.

Tosh ignored him. "The good news is that the power source will last another few thousand years, if I understand these readouts correctly. The bad news is that some of the wiring connections are loose. I think that's what's caused the radiation leakage over the years. I should be able to fix them though. I just need a screwdriver. And the ability not to breathe for five minutes."

"And after that," Jack said grimly, "the five of us are going to steal this thing and send it back through the Rift, away from this planet."

Gwen looked around at the hotel atrium, at the bar and the restaurant seating areas, at the rising series of balconies that looked down on them, and at the penthouse right at the top where presumably Dimitri Arkanovitch, Russian crime boss, was located. "And how exactly are we going to do that without being noticed?" she asked.

"I don't know," Jack replied. "But I'm sure it'll be a work of art." 🐝

TORCHWOOD SERIES 2

COMPLETE EPISODE GUIDE

2.1: KISS KISS, BANG BANG

CREDITS & DATES

CREDITED CAST Captain Jack Harkness **John Barrowman**, Gwen Cooper **Eve Myles**, Owen Harper **Burn Gorman**, Toshiko Sato **Naoko Mori**, Ianto Jones **Gareth David-Lloyd**, Captain John Hart **James Marsters**, Rhys **Kai Owen**, PC Andy Davidson **Tom Price**, Menna Trussler **Old Woman**, Blowfish **Paul Kasey**, Mugger **Crispin Layfield**, Mugger's Victim **Nathan Ryan**, Hologram Woman **Inika Leigh Wright**, Teenage Girl **Sarah Whyte**

WRITER Chris Chibnall
DIRECTOR Ashley Way
PRODUCER Richard Stokes
EXECUTIVE PRODUCERS Russell T Davies and Julie Gardner

BROADCAST DATES
First shown BBC2 16 January 2008
Pre-watershed edit first shown BBC2 23 January 2008

FILMING BLOCK
Three: 6 July 2008-9 August 2008

PLOT SYNOPSIS

Torchwood are in pursuit of a Blowfish in a sports car. They are doing their best to cope without Jack, who disappeared some time before. The team corner the bipedal fish in a suburban house, where it takes a hostage and taunts them, until it is shot – by Jack!

Back at the Hub, Gwen confronts Jack over his disappearance, and he says he came back to be with the team. Meanwhile in the autopsy room, a device pulses in the dead Blowfish's pocket.

On the roof of a car park, a man steps casually out of the Rift and kills a knife-wielding mugger. He then sends Jack a holographic message via his wristband, and Jack goes to meet him, alone. Jack and the man meet, kiss passionately, then fight. The man is another former Time Agent, going by the name of Captain John Hart. The rest of the team arrive at the bar, and John tells them he is there to locate three radiation cluster bombs that have been scattered around Cardiff.

The team agree to help John, but Jack tells Gwen not to trust him. She was in charge while Jack was away, and has also got engaged to her boyfriend Rhys, leading to tension between her and Jack.

The group splits into pairs and Gwen and John find the first in a cargo container. John kisses Gwen with paralysing lipgloss, leaving her to die. Tosh and Owen locate the second device in a warehouse, but again John arrives to incapacitate them.

> ### TUNE!
> The first song to feature in series two of Torchwood is the Prodigy mix of Release Yo'Self by Method Man, which the Blowfish is playing in the sports car.

As Jack and Ianto search an office for the third bomb, Jack asks Ianto on a date. When he goes to search the roof, John arrives and sends Ianto off to save the others. John joins Jack on the roof, with the third device. He admits that they are not bombs at all, before pushing Jack to his death.

Ianto locates the others, and with the revived Jack they confront John in the Hub. He assembles the 'bombs' and the item from the Blowfish to reveal the location of a diamond, but instead it becomes a real bomb, which affixes to his chest.

John forces the team to save him by handcuffing himself to Gwen with a deadlock-seal. Owen injects John with a sample of the team's DNA, to release the bomb from John's body, and Jack hurls it into the Rift. As John leaves, he tells a shocked Jack that he has found someone called Gray...

TORCHWOOD DECLASSIFIED 2.1 First shown BBC2 23 January 2008
Interviewees: John Barrowman, Chris Chibnall, Russell T Davies, Tom Lucy (stunt coordinator), James Marsters, Curtis Rivers (John Barrowman's stunt double), Richard Stokes, Ashley Way

Bringing in a (potentially) one-off guest star to live up to the publicity promise that Torchwood series two would be "punchier, pacier and funnier" was always going to be a gamble. As rogue Time Agent Captain John, James Marsters more than fits the glitzy bill, but where do you go once the character is gone? And what does it say for the regular cast, if they can't be funnier and sexier on their own?

Happily though, any such doubts were quickly dispelled as Captain John proved not to be a distraction from the established Torchwood team, but a worthy foil, and a dark mirror for their returning leader. The show had never seen a full-on, swaggering sci-fi villain before, and John gave the team a focal point to spar with and to fight against, instead of bickering among themselves. And where Jack had often been a shadowy figure in the first series, here John served to define him, by being all the things that Jack had turned his back on.

With Torchwood acting more like a team than ever, there was even time for some reflective moments away from the main action, which confidently set out a path for the series. As Owen and Tosh talked about relationships and settling down, Gwen was living that life, with her engagement to Rhys, after he popped the question while Jack was away. Even Jack, the eternal flirt, was through with messing around with Ianto, and finally got round to asking him out on a proper date, after hints

of a casual relationship in series one. Only time would tell which members of the team would still be together by this series' end.

But the revelation that would have most impact on the series was the closing one – Captain John's enigmatic claim that he had found someone called "Gray" – accompanied by a brief flashback of a child's hand, slipping away. Though the exact repercussions of that news were a long way away, it was instantly clear that John was coming back – and thanks to his villainy, so were our heroes.

CONTINUITY & TRIVIA

■ The opening sequence with the Blowfish was written by Russell T Davies, who then told Chris Chibnall to write an episode following on from it!

■ The original title for the episode was Separation Anxiety.

■ The eventual title, Kiss Kiss, Bang Bang, comes from a 1960s Italian nickname for James Bond, Mr Kiss Kiss, Bang Bang. The critic Pauline Kael called the phrase "perhaps the briefest statement imaginable of the basic appeal of movies."

■ The car driven by the Blowfish is a Chrysler Crossfire.

■ Captain John's line, "Hungry now," line is a knowing reference to Vampire Willow's line "Bored Now," in the Buffy The Vampire Slayer episode The Wish. His line, "You live in the sculpture? Could you be any more pretentious?" is also very redolent of Buffyspeak.

■ When John abandons Gwen at the docks, the wide shot of cargo crates echoes the closing shot of Raiders Of The Lost Ark.

■ The diamond Captain John is seeking comes from Arcadia, mentioned in the 2006 Doctor Who episode Doomsday.

FIRST DRAFT

■ Captain John Hart was called Captain John Hammond at first.

■ The weapons secreted about John's person were to include a blowpipe with poisoned thorns in the front of his trousers.

■ Rhys originally proposed to Gwen at the end of the episode, but Russell T Davies considered it more poignant if it happened off-screen, while Jack was away.

■ Jack and Owen were going to ride a scooter to the rooftop at the end of the story, but would have needed crash helmets.

4.22m

BARB final rating for 16 January broadcast, in millions

2.2: SLEEPER

CREDITS & DATES

CREDITED CAST Captain Jack Harkness **John Barrowman**, Gwen Cooper **Eve Myles**, Owen Harper **Burn Gorman**, Toshiko Sato **Naoko Mori**, Ianto Jones **Gareth David-Lloyd**, Beth **Nikki Amuka-Bird**, Mike **Dyfed Potter**, David **Doug Rollins**, David's wife **Claire Cage**, Mr Grainger **Sean Carlson**, Mrs Grainger **Victoria Pugh**, Burglar 1 **Luke Rutherford**, Burglar 2 **Alex Harries**, Police officer **Dominic Coleman**, Weevil **Paul Kasey**, Boy **William Hughes**, Girl **Millie Philippart**, Driver **Matthew Arwel Pegram**, Paramedic **Derek Lea**

WRITER James Moran
DIRECTOR Colin Teague
PRODUCER Richard Stokes
EXECUTIVE PRODUCERS Russell T Davies and Julie Gardner

BROADCAST DATES
First shown BBC2 23 January 2008
Pre-watershed edit first shown BBC2 24 January 2008

FILMING BLOCK
Two: 3 June 2008-5 July 2008

PLOT SYNOPSIS

When burglars break into the home of Beth Halloran and her husband, Mike, a struggle ensues and Mike is knocked out. The burglars threaten Beth, but are suddenly terrified. When one of the burglars is subsequently found dead and the other seriously injured, Torchwood are called to shed light on the case.

One of the burglars was stabbed with a long blade, but there are no weapons around. When the other burglar wakes in hospital, he says Beth did it, then he dies. When Torchwood interrogate Beth, a light shorts out and Tosh registers an electromagnetic build-up. When Owen tries to take a blood sample, he finds he cannot break her skin. Jack asks Beth what planet she's from, and shows her a Weevil, which visibly cowers before her. The team subject Beth to a mind probe, which penetrates her human persona to reveal an alien soldier within. They discover a transceiver and a forcefield generator in her arm, before Jack realises Beth is a sleeper agent for Cell 114, an alien preparing to invade Earth by stealth.

Beth is devastated to learn that her life is a lie, and agrees to be frozen using cryogenics. The team disables her arm transceiver with an electromagnetic pulse, but this sends a signal which causes other Cell agents to activate. When the Hub goes dark, the team realise Beth has escaped – her deactivated transceiver and reduced life signs a false image all along. Her human side to the fore, Beth goes to the hospital to see Mike, but is horrified when her arm transforms into a huge blade, fatally stabbing him.

Elsewhere, other sleepers are causing chaos – their target a nuclear weapons base outside the city. Jack, Gwen and Beth head for the site, where another Cell member is attacking the defences. Jack runs him down in the SUV, and Gwen successfully disable his forcefield. He tells Jack that the invasion has already begun, before blowing himself up, defeated.

At the Hub, Torchwood prepare to freeze Beth once more, but she does not want to risk hurting anyone else. Her forcefield deactivated, she takes Gwen hostage, forcing the team to gun her down. They are all aware that she has sacrificed herself.

ERM...

Why does Cell 114 need suicide bombers? Their claim to world domination would be considerably stronger if they didn't keep blowing themselves up.

TORCHWOOD DECLASSIFIED 2.2 First shown BBC2 24 January 2008
Interviewees: Nikki Amuka-Bird, John Barrowman, Russell T Davies, Danny Hargreaves (Any Effects), James Moran, Eve Myles, Richard Stokes, Colin Teague.

ANALYSIS

After the outlandish exploits of episode one, Sleeper starts off like a much more traditional tale, that could easily have sat amid Torchwood series one. But while the first few minutes are dark and intense, they are skilfully undercut by James Moran's playful dialogue, and the story quickly expands from domestic procedural to all-out invasion epic.

At the heart of the story is Gwen's friendship with the deceptively timid Beth, played to perfection by Nikki Amuka-Bird. As with the best of Torchwood's first series, these deeply human vignettes ground the scenes of alien action amid a world that is recognisably our own. Though the wider threat is too big to contain within a 50-minute television episode, the focus here is on Nikki's desire to see her husband one last time, and the philosophy and ethics of treating her like an assassin, when her constructed personality is as real as any of our own.

When the all-action climax does kick in, it initially feels like a distraction from Nikki's more emotional plight (we are not invited to feel any sympathy for the other sleeper agents, or their families), but some impressive stunt work and a mix of physical and CG effects make for a worthwhile diversion into mini-movie territory. Jack gets to be every inch the "dashing hero on the case" he claims to be, and for the second time in as many episodes, the entire team pulls together with humour and strength in the face of potential catastrophe. Jack's use of the CB radio is exactly the kind of timeless ingenuity he so admires in the Doctor, and the team he sought to build in the Time Lord's image is shaping up well into just that mould.

By the time we get to Beth's last intimate exchange with Gwen, an awful lot has taken place, but the story never loses sight of the frightened young woman at its heart. When she forces the team to shoot her, in a final act of self sacrifice, it's not so much a tragedy, as a triumph of her humanity, proving more powerful than the killer instincts she was born with. And if the Cell do return, that's why we'll beat them.

CONTINUITY & TRIVIA

■ The Weevils makes their first appearance this series, courtesy of 'Janet', Torchwood's captive specimen.

■ Sean Carlson, who plays Patrick Grainger, previously appeared as a policeman in the 2005 Doctor Who Christmas special, The Christmas Invasion. William Hughes, who plays the Graingers' son, portrayed the young version of the Master in the 2007 Doctor Who episode The Sound Of Drums.

■ Nikki Amuka-Bird used her blade arm prosthetic to play air guitar between takes!

■ Beth is put into cryogenic vault 007, the same location as Suzie Costello and seemingly everyone else stored in the vaults up to this point...

■ Writer James Moran was influenced by the Terminator and Jason Bourne movies, as well as the Cybermen from Doctor Who when he came up with the idea of Cell 114.

■ Moran also wrote The Fires Of Pompeii, the second episode of Doctor Who series four.

■ Kai Owen is credited, but does not appear in the episode.

FIRST DRAFT

■ One early idea for the episode featured a character who didn't know she was an alien coming to the attention of Torchwood through her clairvoyant abilities.

■ The blade in Beth's arm was originally intended to emerge from between the character's knuckles, akin to Wolverine's claws in The X-Men.

■ Ianto had fewer lines in the original script, but writer James Moran was so impressed by Gareth David-Lloyd's comic timing that he quickly added more dialogue for him.

3.78m
BARB final rating for 23 January broadcast, in millions

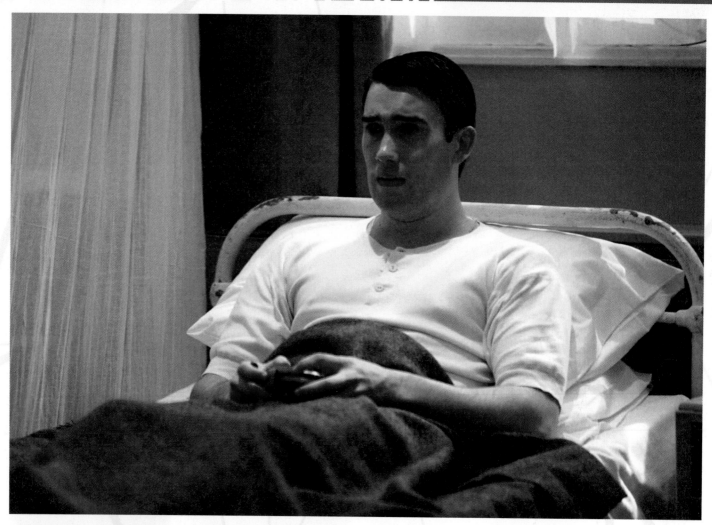

CREDITS & DATES

CREDITED CAST Captain Jack Harkness **John Barrowman**, Gwen Cooper **Eve Myles**, Owen Harper **Burn Gorman**, Toshiko Sato **Naoko Mori**, Ianto Jones **Gareth David-Lloyd**, Rhys Williams **Kai Owen**, Tommy Brockless **Anthony Lewis**, Gerald Carter **Roderic Culver**, Harriet Derbyshire **Siobhan Hewlett**, Nurse **Lizzie Rogan**, Foreman **Ricky Fearon**

WRITER Helen Raynor
DIRECTOR Andy Goddard
PRODUCER Richard Stokes
EXECUTIVE PRODUCERS Russell T Davies and Julie Gardner

BROADCAST DATES
First shown BBC2 30 January 2008
Pre-watershed edit first shown BBC2 31 January 2008

FILMING BLOCK
One: 30 April 2008-31 May 2008

PLOT SYNOPSIS

In 1918, a man and woman take readings in a military hospital. Hearing a rumbling sound, they find Tosh with a soldier they have just seen in the wards above. The soldier tells the pair they must take him from the ward. Realising they have seen the future, they take the shellshocked soldier, Tommy, away from the ward. When he asks who they are, the man says: Torchwood.

In the present day, Jack tells Gwen about Tommy, who Torchwood still hold in cryogenic stasis. They know that they will need him one day, so, once a year, they wake him up.

Tosh arrives in a dress and a very good mood, in time to for Tommy to be revived. She has the day marked as special on her calendar. When Tommy wakes, she is on hand to look after him.

Jack tells Gwen that on an unspecified date in the future, a time-shift will occur, and 1918 will start to co-exist with the present. In 1918, Torchwood left sealed orders, explaining just what Tommy has to do. Tosh takes Tommy out in Cardiff, and it's clear she is attracted to him.

Gwen goes to the hospital where the time-shift will take place. It is due to be demolished, which has caused the time-shift to begin.

In town, Tosh and Tommy play pool and share a drink. Tommy tells Tosh he would do anything for her, and she invites him back to her flat. But Jack summons the pair back to the Hub. Shortly afterwards, the sealed orders unlock.

TUNE!
Tosh starts her day to the sound of Moby's One Of These Mornings, featuring the lyric: "One of these mornings, you will look for me, and I'll be gone."

They say Tommy has to go back to 1918 to seal the rift in time.

Tosh asks Jack what happens to Tommy, and learns that he will be shot for cowardice when his shellshock returns in 1918. She says she cannot send him back, but Jack says she can, and shows her a sketch of herself – part of the sealed orders from 1918.

Tosh and Tommy spend the night together, and he deduces he will die in the war. The next day, he panics, but Tosh convinces him to deliver the message seen by Torchwood in 1918, before he returns to his hospital bed, holding a key to end the time-shift.

Shellshocked once more, Tommy doesn't use the key. Tosh volunteers to enter his mind as a projection in time, and they share a final moment, before he activates the key. Tosh is devastated, but knows that Tommy's sacrifice has saved the world.

TORCHWOOD DECLASSIFIED 2.3 First shown BBC2 31 January 2008
Interviewees: John Barrowman, Chris Chibnall, Russell T Davies, Andy Goddard, Anthony Lewis, Naoko Mori, Helen Raynor.

From the moment that the plummy-voiced ghost hunters reveal themselves to be Torchwood, you know you're in for a treat with To The Last Man. Revisiting themes of time-crossed love touched upon in two of the first series' most popular episodes (Out Of Time and Captain Jack Harkness), this story goes further by making Tosh and Tommy's romance central to the resolution of the threat McGuffin posed by the time shift.

For the third episode in a row, the story is driven by a single guest character, albeit to utterly different effect every time. Anthony Lewis acquits himself well as the dishy but disoriented Tommy, and easily slips between grounded grown-up and terrified country lad in a way that befits someone forced into war at such an early age.

Sharing centre-stage with Tommy, for the first time this series, is Naoko Mori, who gets to expand upon the livelier Tosh we first saw finding Captain John

attractive in Kiss Kiss, Bang Bang. Though still shy and retiring, she has an extra sense of determination here, and is willing to stand up to Jack more than once during the episode. From the energy and anticipation she brings to the first scene in her flat, to the conflict of emotions across her face in the final shot, the actress proves there is much more to Tosh than just gadgets and gizmos.

Away from the central love story, Eve Myles excels as Gwen in the haunted hospital scenes, conveying a wealth of emotions almost entirely without dialogue. These scenes, like the whole episode, benefit greatly from Andy Goddard's excellent direction, and are some of the most memorably eerie moments in the entire series. Redolent of 1970s fantasy show Sapphire And Steel, they are all the better for being shot in daytime. Now if only we could see more of Gerald and Harriet!

FIRST DRAFT

■ Tommy was to enquire after Suzie, meaning Suzie Costello, the former Torchwood second-in-command who would have been on hand last time Tommy was defrosted. Suzie committed suicide in the first episode of series one, Everything Changes, and was herself sealed in the vaults, then later revived.

■ Writer Helen Raynor's original idea saw Tommy revealed to be a soldier from the future, and not the First World War, as the Torchwood team believed. This twist was removed because it made the story too complicated, and caused the team to look as if they had made a big mistake when labelling Tommy's body!

You can help

YOUR COUNTRY NEEDS YOU

CONTINUITY & TRIVIA

■ The episode was originally scheduled as episode four.

■ A working title for the story was A Soldier's Heart, a term for shellshock used in the American Civil War.

■ The actual title refers to Field Marshal Haig's Special Order Of The Day on 11th April 1918: "There is no other course open to us but to fight it out. Every position must be held to the last man: there must be no retirement. With our backs to the wall and believing in the justice of our cause, each one of us must fight on to the end."

■ Owen warns Tosh not to get too close to Tommy, a lesson he learned from his experience with his own anachronistic lover, Diane in Out Of Time.

■ Tommy comments on the ridiculousness of saving the world in his pyjamas, though the Doctor did just that in the 2005 Doctor Who special, The Christmas Invasion.

■ Jack and Ianto share their first on-screen kiss of the series. The first of several!

■ Kai Owen is credited, but does not appear in the episode.

3.51m

BARB final rating for 30 January broadcast, in millions

2.4: MEAT

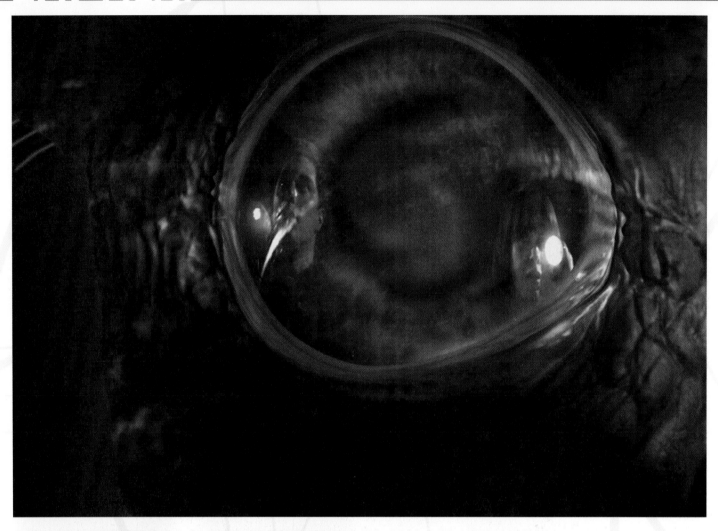

CREDITS & DATES

CREDITED CAST Captain Jack Harkness **John Barrowman**, Gwen Cooper **Eve Myles**, Owen Harper **Burn Gorman**, Toshiko Sato **Naoko Mori**, Ianto Jones **Gareth David-Lloyd**, Rhys Williams **Kai Owen**, Policeman **Colin Baxter**, Ruth **Patti Clare**, Vic **Garry Lake**, Greg **Gerard Carey**, Dale **Matt Ryan**

WRITER Catherine Tregenna
DIRECTOR Colin Teague
PRODUCER Richard Stokes
EXECUTIVE PRODUCERS
Russell T Davies and Julie Gardner

BROADCAST DATES
First shown BBC2 6 February 2008
Pre-watershed edit first shown
BBC2 7 February 2008

FILMING BLOCK
Two: 3 June 2008–5 July 2008

PLOT SYNOPSIS

Gwen's fiancé Rhys gets a call to say that one of the lorries from Harwood's, the haulage firm he works for, has crashed. Arriving on the scene, he's shocked to find the driver dead, and Gwen is among the 'special ops' team sent in to investigate the suspicious cargo of meat he was carrying.

The team soon discover that the meat is not from Earth, and Tosh calls Rhys, posing as a police officer, to ask what Harwood's knows about it. He is forced to admit he has no details for the firm behind the delivery, but Gwen refuses to suspect him.

Torchwood tracks the meat's source to a warehouse in Merthyr, and Rhys follows them to the location, after Gwen tells him she knows nothing about the crash.

The team prepare to storm the warehouse, but hold off when they see Rhys going in.

Spotted by the gang in charge at the warehouse, Rhys has to bluff his way in with their leader, Dale, claiming that he wants to take over deliveries where his dead colleague left off. Dale shows Rhys the source of the meat – a huge whale-like creature, howling in pain. No matter how much they cut, says Dale, it just keeps getting bigger.

Back at their flat, Rhys confronts Gwen. When she tells him about Torchwood, he tells her to prove it.

Gwen takes Rhys to the Hub, where Jack barracks him for jeopardising their operation. Rhys points out he has found them a way in, as their new delivery driver. Gwen disagrees, but Jack overrules her.

At the warehouse, Rhys keeps the gang busy while Torchwood get in. They team are shocked by what they see, and realise that the animal is sentient.

As the team overpower the workers, Ianto is spotted and Dale takes him and Rhys hostage. With the team discovered, Jack tells Dale that the creature is an alien, fallen through the Rift. Angry and confused, Dale tries to shoot Gwen, but Rhys takes the bullet. Ianto grapples with Dale, who fires again, hitting the whale.

Panicked, the creature breaks its bonds and traps Jack, Tosh, Gwen and Rhys. Ianto takes out the gang with a taser, while Owen is forced to put the creature out of its misery.

Later, Jack tells Gwen she must retcon Rhys, but she refuses, and he retains his knowledge of Torchwood.

ERM...
Rhys' mobile phone has the same ringtone as Gwen's in Kiss Kiss, Bang Bang. That's sweet, but it's probably not ideal for a co-habiting couple...

TORCHWOOD DECLASSIFIED 2.4 First shown BBC2 7 February 2008
Interviewees: Barney Curnow (The Mill), Russell T Davies, Eve Myles, Kai Owen, Richard Stokes, Colin Teague, Catherine Tregenna.

ANALYSIS

Sooner or later, Rhys was going to have to find out about Torchwood, and, happily, it happened sooner, just four episodes in to the second series. If Gwen had kept her fiancé in the dark much longer, she would have come across as two-faced, and he would have seemed like a fool. Instead, bringing him in on the secret opens up a whole new side of Rhys – and a fresh world of storylines for the couple with no more secrets.

Kai Owen really makes the most of his expanded role as Rhys, echoing Gwen's own awe at seeing the Hub in the first series, and locking horns with Jack in true Alpha Male fashion. Rhys proves himself to be just as brave and reliable as any of the 'official' Torchwood team, and it's clear for the first time just why Gwen loves him so much. The fact that he has no appetite for the hero lifestyle full-time just adds to his everyman appeal.

But it's when Gwen and Rhys fight that this episode really captures what Torchwood is all about, and does so with a visceral realism that makes it a highlight of the series. Eve Myles and Kai Owen are utterly believable as a rowing couple in love – furious but terrified of losing each other – and the fantastical subject matter ("Aliens? In Cardiff?") makes the exchange as funny as it is affecting. Against that back-drop, the computer generated alien whale itself could be almost peripheral, but the sheer vastness conjured up by The Mill makes it something of a showstopper in its own right. Completely different from any other CG effect seen in either Torchwood or Doctor Who, and lacking any of the human features usually considered necessary to evoke sympathy for a alien, it's testament to everyone involved that the creature's plight is quite so moving.

Add the sight of Jack flirting with Rhys' staff in a Portakabin, and Meat is possibly the series highlight so far.

CONTINUITY & TRIVIA

■ Catherine Tregenna also wrote the following episode, Adam, and the series one episodes Out Of Time and Captain Jack Harkness. That makes her the second most prolific Torchwood writer after Chris Chibnall, who has eight episodes to his name.

■ Rhys got the job as manager of Harwood's Haulage in Kiss Kiss, Bang Bang. His call to tell Gwen the news allowed Tosh to track her location later on.

■ Tosh makes sandwiches for Owen in a bid to spend some time with him, but in the next episode, Adam, it's the alternate version of Owen who is making sandwiches for Tosh.

■ Gwen's line, "What is this, Scooby-Doo?" when Rhys says they can hide in the back of his van is possibly a knowing reference to Guardian reviewer Charlie Brooker's affectionate take on the series.

■ Owen's line, "I'm so sorry," when he puts the whale out of its misery echoes the use of the phrase in Doctor Who.

■ Gwen refuses to retcon Rhys this series, though she did so in series one's Combat, after she confessed her affair with Owen.

FIRST DRAFT

■ When Russell T Davies first suggested a story based around a giant alien whale, Catherine Tregenna and the script team considered making it a fabulous and exotic creature. But they decided to make it a sentient slab of meat when they realised anything more fantastical would be exploited as a King-Kong style tourist attraction, rather than harvested for its meat.

■ Rhys was originally going to stay dead at the end of series one, after he was stabbed by Bilis Manger, but survived for an expanded role in series two.

3.28m
BARB final rating for 6 February broadcast, in millions

2.5: ADAM

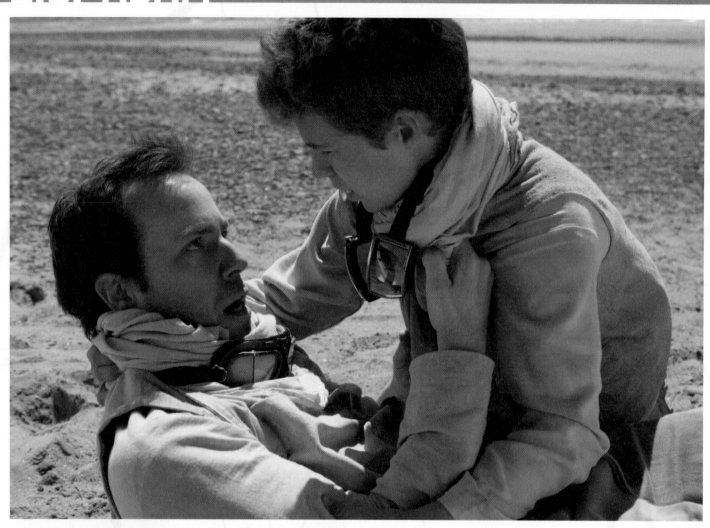

CREDITS & DATES

CREDITED CAST Captain Jack Harkness **John Barrowman**, Gwen Cooper **Eve Myles**, Owen Harper **Burn Gorman**, Toshiko Sato **Naoko Mori**, Ianto Jones **Gareth David-Lloyd**, Rhys Williams **Kai Owen**, Adam Smith **Bryan Dick**, Weevil **Paul Kasey**, Jack's Father **Demetri Goritsas**, Jack's Mother **Lauren Ward**, Young Jack **Jack Montgomery**, Gray **Ethan Brooke**, Young Adam **Rhys Myers**, Youth **Lloyd Everitt**, Dead Woman **Jo McLaren**

WRITER Catherine Tregenna
DIRECTOR Andy Goddard
PRODUCER Richard Stokes
EXECUTIVE PRODUCERS
Russell T Davies and Julie Gardner

BROADCAST DATES
First shown BBC2 13 February 2008
Pre-watershed edit first shown
BBC2 14 February 2008

FILMING BLOCK
One: 30 April 2008–31 May 2008

PLOT SYNOPSIS

Gwen returns from a weekend away to find the team in the Hub – Jack, Owen, Tosh, Ianto and Adam. Gwen says she has no idea who Adam is, but a touch on the shoulder reminds her of their friendship, and they laugh together. As Adam updates his personnel file, Tosh asks where an alien box in the Hub came from. Adam kisses her. They've been together for a year.

Gwen returns home and pulls a gun on Rhys, who she believes to be an intruder. Jack arrives with Adam, and finds she has no memory of her fiance. Rhys is left angry and upset.

Later, Jack starts to see visions from his childhood, and Adam tells him to confide in him. Jack remembers fleeing from a race of aliens as they attack his home planet in the 51st Century. Jack tries to keep his little brother Gray safe, but he loses hold of his hand. He tells Adam that he never found his brother again.

Ianto checks his diary to see if he made a record of the box Tosh was asking about. He is surprised to find no mention of Adam in his diary at all. Adam's form flickers, and he attacks Ianto, saying he exists by feeding himself into people's memories. As Ianto struggles, Adam makes him believe he is a serial killer.

In Gwen's flat, Rhys is slowly winning back Gwen's confidence, as she remembers more about their relationship.

In the Hub, Ianto is tormented by his false memories, and confesses to Jack, who hooks him up to a lie detector. It says Ianto is telling the truth, but Jack refuses to believe it. He checks the Hub's security footage and sees Adam implanting memories in the teams' minds.

Jack holds Adam at gunpoint, and tells the team the truth about their 'friend's' secret, much to everyone's shock and Tosh's distress. Adam admits he was drawn to their unique memories, implanting himself in their minds to survive.

Jack gathers the team and gives them each a retcon pill so they can forget Adam and escape his influence. It is hardest for Tosh – who is very much in love.

Adam offers Jack one last happy memory of his father and Gray, but makes himself part of the memory, forcing Jack to forget it, if he is to erase Adam, too. Reluctantly, Jack takes the retcom, and Adam is gone.

TUNE!

As Gwen and Rhys wrestle in bed at the start of the episode, Magazine's version of the Captain Beefheart track I Love You Big Dummy plays on the radio.

TORCHWOOD DECLASSIFIED 2.5 First shown BBC2 14 February 2008
Interviewees: John Barrowman, Gareth David-Lloyd, Russell T Davies, Bryan Dick, Andy Goddard, Demetri Goritsas, Ray Holman (costume designer), Richard Stokes, Catherine Tregenna

Sleeping with his co-workers, and keeping secrets, it's no wonder Adam found it easy to blend in at Torchwood for a while! Adam took a well established sci-fi trope – the alternative world of 'What-if?' – and ran with it in new and interesting directions. Such a set-up allows writer Catherine Tregenna to have a lot of fun with the characters we know and love, but also to explore some deeper truths beneath the simple novelty value.

We learn that Owen's closed-off nature is related to his difficult relationship with his mother, and that Tosh's loneliness is what holds her back. Ianto can never really forget his lost love, Lisa, and Gwen will always love Jack, no matter what her feelings for Rhys.

But it's the insights into Jack's usually very private life that are the biggest revelations here. Gray, first mentioned back in Kiss Kiss, Bang Bang, is revealed not to be a father, lover or long-lost son, as fans had speculated, but Jack's little brother, left behind and seemingly lost forever in the harsh sand dunes of the Boeshane Peninsula. Who could know that these events on a far-off world in the 51st Century would eventually lead to the death of Tosh and the end for Owen?

Jack's homeworld itself is a triumph of location filming and (relatively) simple CGI. The unforgiving landscape and costumes have echoes of Tatooine in Star Wars: very definitely the sort of place where heroes are first made.

Adam himself is more than just a necessary conduit for these fan-pleasing insights, too. Played with insidious subtlty by Bryan Dick, the character is needy and conflicted, planting benign and pleasant memories to begin with, before escalating to false remembrances of murder and torture, without ever facing up to the consequences of what he does to survive. The effect he has on Ianto is especially harrowing, and proves Gareth David-Lloyd can do much more than just wisecracking.

When Jack and Ianto finally realise the truth about Adam, the team's collective healing process is almost religious, as Jack hands out retcon like a kind of Communion. But this is no reset button, as everyone's story arc moves on apace, and we wait to find out whatever happened to Gray...

CONTINUITY & TRIVIA

■ Shots of Adam are intercut with the standard opening montage, a device also used in the Buffy The Vampire Slayer episode Superstar.

■ The working title for the episode was Memory Adam.

■ The Torchwood novel Border Princes by Dan Abnett features an alien who changes the team's memories to infiltrate their ranks.

■ We see Jack's childhood home, the Boeshane Peninsula, for the first time, after it was mentioned in the 2007 Doctor Who episode The Last Of The Time Lords.

■ We also see Jack's little brother Gray for the first time, after a glimpse of his (unidentified) hand in flashback at the end of Kiss Kiss, Bang Bang.

■ Jack's father was called Franklin. His mother appears, but is not named.

■ Ianto recalls meeting and losing Lisa, his late girlfriend, seen in the first series episodes Cyberwoman and End Of Days.

■ The scene where Gwen pulls a gun on Rhys was the first to be shot for series two.

FIRST DRAFT

■ Russell T Davies asked writer Catherine Tregenna to expand upon the background of Jack's childhood in the 51st Century Boeshane Peninsula, which was a small part of her original story outline.

■ The episode was initially planned to run much later in the series, so Gwen and Rhys were already married when Adam made Gwen forget who Rhys was. Jack subsequently pointed out the wedding ring on Gwen's finger when she was pointing her gun at Rhys in their flat.

3.79m

BARB final rating for 13 February broadcast, in millions

2.6: RESET

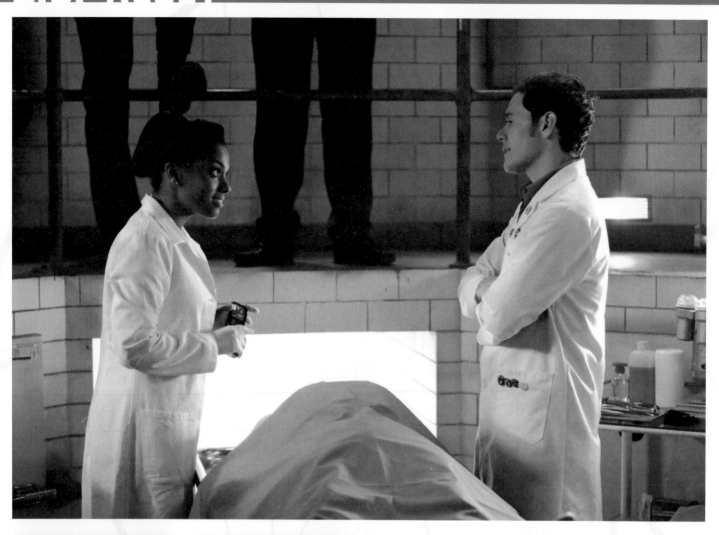

CREDITS & DATES

CREDITED CAST Captain Jack Harkness **John Barrowman**, Gwen Cooper **Eve Myles**, Owen Harper **Burn Gorman**, Toshiko Sato **Naoko Mori**, Ianto Jones **Gareth David-Lloyd**, Martha Jones **Freema Agyeman**, Aaron Copley **Alan Dale**, Plummer **Jacqueline Boatswain**, Marie Thomas **Jan Anderson**, Billy Davis **Rhodri Miles**, Mike **Michael Sewell**, Policeman **John Samuel Worsey**

WRITER JC Wilsher
DIRECTOR Ashley Way
PRODUCER Richard Stokes
EXECUTIVE PRODUCERS
Russell T Davies and Julie Gardner

BROADCAST DATES
First shown BBC3 13 February 2008
Repeated BBC2 20 February 2008
Pre-watershed edit first shown
BBC2 21 February 2008

FILMING BLOCK
Three: 6 July 2008-9 August 2008

PLOT SYNOPSIS

As Owen performs an autopsy on a mystery body, Ianto tells Jack he has a VIP guest. It is Martha Jones, now working as a UNIT doctor. She points out something Owen has missed on the body: a tiny puncture on one eyeball, through which the body has been pumped full of ammonium hydroxide. Martha is investigating a series of similar deaths, centred around South Wales.

Jack gives Martha a tour of the Hub, and she notices an artefact Owen calls the singularity scalpel, which, if used properly, can vaporise objects and not harm anything in between. Ianto reports there has been another attack, but this time the victim has survived.

Owen and Martha visit the woman who was attacked, and realise the ammonium hydroxide is being used to hide something in the victims' blood. She reveals she had HIV, before she was 'cured' by a drug called Reset, which she was given at a clinic called the Pharm. She begins to spasm suddenly, and dies. A swarm of insects flies out of her mouth, then drop to the ground, dead.

Owen and Martha discover that Reset is a miracle cure-all that comes at a price: alien insects incubating in the patient's body. Jack and Owen visit the Pharm, where its director, Professor Copley, denies any knowledge of Reset. Martha volunteers to go undercover as a trial subject, and she helps Tosh download all the Pharm's data on the parasite,

which they call the Mayfly. An adult Mayfly escapes into the grounds, and Martha is sedated by armed guards pursuing it.

Gwen and Ianto track down an assassin for the Pharm, and Jack interrogates him. He begins to cough up blood, and when Owen uses the singularity scalpel on him, a Mayfly bursts from the man's stomach, killing him.

At the Pharm, Copley quizzes Martha about her unique metabolism, which shows she has travelled in time. He injects her with Reset, and a Mayfly begins to grow inside her. Torchwood arrive in time to save Martha, but Owen is forced to use the singularity scalpel again. She survives, but Copley escapes. As the team begin to shut down the Pharm, Copley appears with a gun, and shoots Owen. Jack shoots Copley, but it is too late. Owen is dead.

> ### ERM...
> If the team can speak to Martha directly through the contact lenses, rather than texting, "in an emergency", why do they need the text facility at all?

TORCHWOOD DECLASSIFIED 2.6 First shown BBC2 20 February 2008
Interviewees: Freema Agyeman, John Barrowman, Mike Crowley, Alan Dale, Gareth David-Lloyd, Russell T Davies, Burn Gorman, Richard Stokes, Ashley Way

Martha's introduction to the world of Torchwood was always going to be an event, and one of the first publicity pictures for series two depicted Freema Agyeman and the team months before transmission. In the event however, it was not such a jarring show-stopper as might have been expected, and Martha slipped easily enough into the Torchwood world. That was thanks in part to the medical leanings of the story, but also because her friend Captain Jack was, more than ever, the same irrepressible hero we first met in Doctor Who.

Indeed, the whole story has something of a Doctor Who flavour to it, without ever losing the characteristics that make Torchwood unique, rather than just a straightforward spin-off. Martha fulfils the twin roles of inquisitive investigator and damsel in distress so beloved of the Doctor's companions, which none of the rest of the team could easily have taken; and

in Copley and the Mayfly the episode has a classic misguided scientist villain, as well as an eye-catching 'monster'.

As Copley, guest star Alan Dale makes the most of his limited screen time to create a presence that looms large throughout. Never before has Torchwood faced an opponent with the same access in the corridors of power, and it was exhilarating to see Jack stand up to someone his own size. As in Meat, just two weeks before, Jack takes a stance against the Pharm because it is the morally right thing to do, not simply to protect humanity against the future, though that too is a factor.

At the end of the episode, the dramatic convention of a hero talking down a gunman at close range, with no thought for his own safety, is turned on its head, as Owen is shot dead – without fanfare or build-up. It is all the more shocking as Copley has so far seemed to rely on his "fire-proof" Whitehall protection to get his way, while others do his dirty work.

It is a fleeting final act for Copley, but it sends the series off in a bold and unexpected new direction. Was Owen really dead? Was Martha here to stay? What would it mean for Tosh and the others? Though the 'next time' trailer skilfully kept all those answers a secret, Owen's most dramatic storyline was only just beginning...

FIRST DRAFT

■ Martha did not feature in the earliest drafts of the episode.

■ At the start of the episode, the team originally emerged from the sewers in pursuit of the Weevil.

■ Before Alan Dale was cast as Copley, his colleague Plummer killed Owen at the end.

■ Plummer originally attacked Martha with the singularity scalpel, causing Owen to jump into its path, but Russell T Davies considered a bullet wound to be more obviously final than this more 'sci-fi' manner of death.

CONTINUITY & TRIVIA

■ Freema Agyeman is credited in the opening titles for all three of her episodes.

■ Since we last saw her at the end of Doctor Who series three, Martha Jones has accepted a job with UNIT.

■ UNIT has featured in Doctor Who on and off since 1969. In the first series Torchwood episode Greeks Bearing Gifts, Jack asks Tosh to prepare a list for UNIT.

■ A copy of the Western Mail showing Margaret Blaine, as seen in the 2005 Doctor Who episode Boom Town, is pinned on the door to Torchwood's tourist information facade.

■ Jack's reference to "a bad experience with a politician" refers to Harold Saxon, aka The Master in Doctor Who.

■ Martha's line, "Be invisible? I can do that," is a reference to her use of the perception filter in the 2007 Doctor Who episode The Sound Of Drums.

■ Ben Foster's incidental music incorporates elements of Murray Gold's theme for Martha, as heard in Doctor Who.

■ Ianto reuses the Taser device seen in Meat.

3.22m

BARB final rating for 20 February broadcast, in millions

CREDITS & DATES

CREDITED CAST Captain Jack Harkness **John Barrowman**, Gwen Cooper **Eve Myles**, Owen Harper **Burn Gorman**, Toshiko Sato **Naoko Mori**, Ianto Jones **Gareth David-Lloyd**, Rhys Williams **Kai Owen**, Martha Jones **Freema Agyeman**, Little Girl **Skye Bennett**, Weevil **Paul Kasey**, Nurse **Joanna Griffiths**, Jamie Burton **Ben Walker**, Hen Night Girl **Lauren Phillips**, Doctor **Golda Rosheuvel**, Hospital Patient **Janie Booth**, Police Officer **Rhys Ap William**

WRITER Matt Jones
DIRECTOR Andy Goddard
PRODUCER Richard Stokes
EXECUTIVE PRODUCERS
Russell T Davies and Julie Gardner

BROADCAST DATES
First shown BBC3 20 February 2008
Repeated BBC2 27 February 2008
Pre-watershed edit first shown
BBC2 28 February 2008

FILMING BLOCK
Four: 13 August–14 September 2008

PLOT SYNOPSIS

Martha is about to begin Owen's autopsy, but Jack says he is going to bring him back. He goes to a derelict church where Weevils sleep around a bizarre shrine. At its centre is a glove that can bring people back from the dead. Jack uses the Resurrection Glove on Owen, and the team say their brief goodbyes in the short time that the glove should work. Owen remains conscious however, despite having no medical life signs. Unseen, the glove moves of its own accord.

As Martha runs tests on Owen, he finds himself suddenly alone in a pitch black void, then recovers. Later, his eyes turn black and he speaks in a strange language. He becomes himself again and leaves the Hub. Jack finds Owen in a bar, where he lashes out, and both men are arrested. In a cell, Jack and Owen talk about life and death, and Owen vomits spectacularly. All bodily pleasures are now denied him, including the ability to process food and drink. The pair are released, but are pursued by Weevils. The creatures do not attack, however, but bow down in front of Owen, who changes once again, uttering inhuman words.

The team translate Owen's incantation as "I shall walk the Earth and my hunger will know no bounds." Gwen finds the phrase in a medieval carving, which tells of a young girl who was resurrected, bringing the embodiment of Death to Earth. Only faith was able to stop it. Owen tells the team they should embalm him to stop Death gaining a foothold on Earth. Jack agrees, but when Martha prepares to inject him, the glove comes to life and attacks her. She ages rapidly, and a black cloud emerges from Owen, killing Jack.

The team take Martha to hospital, but Death has followed them, and stalks the corridors. The building is evacuated, but Jamie, a young patient, doesn't hear the alarm. Owen, now free from Death's influence, rescues Jamie from the spectre, before realising he must face it alone, as it was Faith – the resurrected girl – who stopped Death hundreds of years before. He grapples with the figure, but it cannot kill him, as he is already dead. It is consigned back to where it came from, and Martha becomes young again. Owen, meanwhile, is left to reflect on his uncertain future.

TUNE!
The somg playing in the club is *Awfully Deep* by Roots Manuva, featuring the lyric: "I'm seeing things that I don't wanna see, I see the Devil sit right before me."

TORCHWOOD DECLASSIFIED 2.7 First shown BBC2 28 February 2008
Interviewees: Freema Agyeman, John Barrowman, Mike Crowley (special effects supervisor), Russell T Davies, Andy Goddard, Burn Gorman, Pete Hawkins, Matt Jones, Ruari Mears, Richard Stokes.

ANALYSIS

For a show that professed to have a lighter touch this time around, Torchwood risked getting very dark, very quickly with the death of Owen in the middle of the series. Dead Man Walking could easily have been a disheartening and grim experience, but it somehow manages to be a rollicking good fantasy adventure, as well as a meditation on the nature of life and death. Jack's quest for the glove is a wonderfully gothic cut-away that hints at a permanent fantastic underbelly to Cardiff – and the glove's subsequent animation, and the computer generated figure of death are full-on spectacle, which juxtapose well with Owen's philosophical inner torment.

Centre-stage for the first time this series, Burn Gorman gives a typically believable performance in a role with no real precedent to build on. He is both sympathetic and sinister as he comes to terms with his own death, going through the early stages of grief (denial and anger), with a side helping of

possession. It's a sign of the show's growing confidence that the subsequent stages (bargaining, depression, acceptance) are held over to the following week's episode, allowing this most profound of character arcs the space it really needs to breathe – or, in Owen's case, not breathe.

When Owen finally wrestles with death (Ben Foster's theme for the character welling magnificently), it is the culmination of one of the show's recurring themes. Despite its immortal lead character and previous use of the resurrection glove, Torchwood has always been far more explicit about the finality of death than most sci-fi shows, which operate a 'don't ask, don't tell' policy on the afterlife. But when Jack, Owen and Suzie

(in series one) come back from the dead, they remember only bleak, unremitting darkness, where something ominous lurks. Here, at last, is that something, and Owen puts it back in its place.

The possibility that there is nothing more beyond this life is a bleak one, but it makes these characters hungry for life, and eager to live it to the full. Amid the darkness, this episode's lasting message remains a bright one.

FIRST DRAFT

■ Jack originally interrogated a Hoix (as seen in the 2006 Doctor Who episode Love And Monsters, and episode 13, Exit Wounds) to locate the resurrection glove.

■ The young girl who actually directs Jack to the glove was going to have a cigar and a glass of whisky, until executive producer Julie Gardner vetoed the idea!

■ The code for the alien morgue is 231165. In early drafts of the script it is 231163. The date of the first ever transmission of Doctor Who was 23 November 1963.

CONTINUITY & TRIVIA

■ The title of the episode comes from the call of prison guards in America leading condemned men to the electric chair. A book of the same name was adapted for Hollywood in 1995.

■ Dead Man Walking was also the name of the episode of Torchwood Declassified that accompanied Random Shoes in series one, as well as an episode of the first series of Robin Hood.

■ The story is set immediately after the end of Reset. The next episode, A Day In The Death, takes place three days later, putting Dead Man Walking in a very specific timeframe.

■ The resurrection glove forms a pair with the one seen in Everything Changes and They Keep Killing Suzie in series one. Ianto foreshadows its discovery in the latter episode, when he says, "That's the thing about gloves, sir. They come in pairs."

■ The alien translation device from series one is featured.

■ The incantation that Owen recites includes words from Stephen R Donaldson's The Chronicles Of Thomas Covenant, The Unbeliever, a trilogy of fantasy novels. In the books, the words are used as a blessing.

3.31m

BARB final rating for 27 February broadcast, in millions

CREDITS & DATES

CREDITED CAST Captain Jack Harkness **John Barrowman**, Gwen Cooper **Eve Myles**, Owen Harper **Burn Gorman**, Toshiko Sato **Naoko Mori**, Ianto Jones **Gareth David-Lloyd**, Martha Jones **Freema Agyeman**, Henry Parker **Richard Briers**, Maggie **Christine Bottomley**, Farrington **Louis Decosta Johnson**, Taylor **Brett Allen**, Webb **Gil Kolirin**

WRITER Joseph Lidster
DIRECTOR Andy Goddard
PRODUCER Richard Stokes
EXECUTIVE PRODUCERS Russell T Davies and Julie Gardner

BROADCAST DATES
First shown BBC3 27 February 2008
Repeated BBC2 5 March 2008
Pre-watershed edit first shown BBC2 6 March 2008

FILMING BLOCK
Four: 13 August–14 September 2008

PLOT SYNOPSIS

Owen is on a rooftop with a suicidal woman called Maggie. Three days ago he died, and everything changed. He asks Maggie if she's ready to jump, before telling her about his day... Suspended from duty while Martha monitors him, Owen is reduced to making coffee, as the team hold a meeting. They discuss an unusual energy spike at the mansion of Henry Parker, a reclusive collector of alien artefacts.

Later, Owen accidentally slices his hand with a scalpel. As his body can no longer heal itself, he will have to stitch the wound indefinitely. He goes home and clears out the remnants of his life: food, drink and toiletries all now useless. Back on the roof, Maggie tells Owen why she wants to kill herself.

Her husband died a year ago, on their wedding day, and the pain has never gone away. She asks Owen if it gets better when you die. He continues to tell his story.

In his flat, Owen becomes angry and deliberately harms himself in front of Tosh. He runs, and tries to drown himself in Cardiff Bay, but he no longer needs to breathe. Jack meets him at the water's edge and takes him back to the Hub, where the team are preparing to go to Parker's mansion. The building is alarmed with heat sensors, so Owen volunteers for the mission, having no body heat.

At the house, Owen fools the sensors and overcomes the guards before tracing the energy spike to Parker's bedroom. Bedridden and irritated, Parker is gripping the device causing the readings, which he calls the Pulse. Parker is bitter at the thought of dying, and believes the Pulse can keep him alive. In exchange for the device, Owen promises to help Parker face death, but the old man suffers a heart attack. Owen is unable to give him the kiss of life, and he dies. Tosh tells Owen the Pulse is going to explode, and he prepares to absorb the energy.

On the roof, Maggie asks what happened, and Owen takes the Pulse from his bag. Instead of exploding, it 'sang' to him. Ribbons of brilliant coloured light flow from the Pulse, and Owen tells Maggie there is always something worth living for. He didn't come to the roof to jump. He came to help.

ERM...
Whatever could be the root of Owen's dislike of Tintin? The brave young man who seeks out adventure is not too different from Owen himself!

TORCHWOOD DECLASSIFIED 2.8 First shown BBC2 6 March 2008
Interviewees: Richard Briers, Andy Goddard, Burn Gorman, Ray Holman (costume designer), James Leigh (camera operator), Joseph Lidster, Richard Stokes

ANALYSIS

Dealing with the death of a loved one is something we all have to face sooner or later, and most adult TV shows have tackled themes of grief at some time or other. But dealing with the grief of your own death? That's pure Torchwood: giving classic themes a fresh new twist.

It's very much Owen's episode, of course, and his opening narration and linking scenes with Maggie are another departure for the show, which could have played it safe with such sensitive subject matter. Instead, it boldly proves what the format is capable of, without feeling forced or jarring. It also shows that Torchwood has the courage of its convictions: not just killing off a character for mid-season spectacle, but exploring the consequences with thoughtful aplomb.

But the rest of the team are not neglected, and through Owen's eyes we see them in a subtly more subjective way than usual: Tosh as the well-

meaning presence he can't quite focus on; Jack a sometimes distant, not always sympathetic authority figure; Ianto the rising star and seeming usurper; and Gwen and Martha representing the things Owen thinks he can no longer have: emotional happiness and a brilliant career.

The episode also sees Owen confronting himself in more ways than one: Maggie is his suicidal, fatalistic tendency made flesh (sharing a history not too dissimilar from Owen's own, as we later discover in Fragments), while Parker represents his stubborn, jealous hunger for life,

similar to the man Owen might have been, had he lived.

As Parker, Richard Briers is, of course, superb, mixing just the right amount of pathos with wry, cantankerous bitterness, to stop things getting too maudlin or trite. Having lived his life on television, every inch of Briers face is familiar to us, and calls to mind the youth he has so long left behind. Christine Bottomley is also excellent as Maggie, yet neither actor detracts from Burn Gorman's own typically affecting performance.

That this is Joseph Lidster's first TV script just makes its assuredness all the more thrilling.

FIRST DRAFT

■ The Pulse device originally showed Parker an image of his late wife, giving him the strength to carry on. However, it was considered more poignant if the Pulse itself gave Parker hope.

■ Martha and Gwen discussed wedding dresses in one early draft, leaving Owen upset that the team were getting on with their everyday lives.

■ After Owen tries to drown himself in the Bay, Jack originally reeled off some of his own grisly ends, after he first realised that he could not die.

CONTINUITY & TRIVIA

■ Owen's opening narration includes clips from Everything Changes, Ghost Machine and Out Of Time from series one, as well as Meat from series two.

■ This is the second Torchwood episode to feature a deceased narrator telling the story, after series one's Random Shoes.

■ In another link to Random Shoes, Parker is said to own a Dogon eye. According to Jack in that episode, there used to be a trade in them.

■ Owen was previously relieved of his duties in the series one episode End Of Days.

■ Owen says Parker is "mostly harmless", a phrase used by Douglas Adams to describe the Earth in the Hitchhiker's Guide To The Galaxy books.

■ Tosh brings Jubilee Pizzas to Owen's flat. The pizza of choice in the Torchwood and Doctor Who universe, the brand made its first appearance in the 2005 Doctor Who story Dalek.

■ Richard Briers previously played the Chief Caretaker in the 1987 Doctor Who story Paradise Towers.

■ Kai Owen is credited, but does not appear in the episode.

3.08m

BARB final rating for 5 March broadcast, in millions

CREDITS & DATES

CREDITED CAST Captain Jack **John Barrowman**, Gwen **Eve Myles**, Owen **Burn Gorman**, Tosh **Naoko Mori**, Ianto **Gareth David-Lloyd**, Rhys **Kai Owen**, Brenda **Nerys Hughes**, Mary **Sharon Morgan**, Geraint **William Thomas**, Barry **Robin Griffith**, Carrie **Collette Brown**, Megan **Danielle Henry**, Trina **Ceri Ann Gregory**, Banana Boat **Jonathan Lewis Owen**, Mervyn **Morgan Hopkins**, Registrar **Valerie Murray**, Shop Assistant **Pethrow Gooden**

WRITER Phil Ford
DIRECTOR Ashley Way
PRODUCER Richard Stokes
EXECUTIVE PRODUCERS
Russell T Davies and Julie Gardner

BROADCAST DATES
First shown BBC3 5 March 2008
Repeated BBC2 12 March 2008
Pre-watershed edit first shown BBC2 13 March 2008

FILMING BLOCK
Six: 21 October-22 November 2008

PLOT SYNOPSIS

The night before her wedding, Gwen chases a shapeshifting alien which bites her, before Jack kills it. The next morning, she wakes up to find herself heavily pregnant. Owen examines Gwen and tells her she is carrying an alien egg, passed on through the bite. Jack says she should postpone the wedding, but Gwen refuses, saying she's put Rhys through enough already. Owen begins an autopsy on the dead alien, and Jack tells Tosh to keep an eye on Gwen.

At the wedding venue, one of the guests, Mervyn, takes a shine to a woman called Carrie, and pins a flower to her dress, pricking her and drawing blood. They go to his room, and Tosh sees a speck of Carrie's blood, which is black. She pursues them, but is hindered by the oafish best man, Banana Boat.

In the Hub, Owen realises the dead alien is a male Nostrovite, a species that mates for life. When the egg in Gwen's body is ready to hatch, the female will track her down and tear its baby out of her. Jack, Owen and Ianto set off for the wedding, taking the singularity scalpel with them.

Carrie is the female Nostrovite, and she kills Mervyn before Tosh can get to them. Again, Banana Boat distracts Tosh, and Carrie cocoons them both as a snack for later. Owen and Ianto rescue the pair, while Jack interrupts the wedding to warn Gwen of the threat. One of the guests finds Mervyn's remains, and tells everyone he has been murdered.

As the wedding descends into chaos, Jack and Tosh pursue the Nostrovite and Owen tells Gwen and Rhys they must use the singularity scalpel to vaporise the egg in Gwen's body. The Nostrovite takes the form of Rhys' mother and then Jack, but when Gwen and Owen shoot it, bullets have no effect. Jack says they will need a bigger gun.

Owen cannot use the singularity scalpel with his injured hand, so he entrusts it to Rhys, who successfully destroys the egg. The Nostrovite, back in the shape of Rhys' mother, bursts in, but it is too late. Before it can take its revenge, Jack shoots it with a huge alien rifle.

Finally, Gwen and Rhys marry, and Jack retcons all the guests at the reception, but the newlyweds refuse amnesia pills for themselves.

> **TUNE!**
> Super Furry Animals sing "I've got a butterfly stomach for you," in Fire In My Heart, as Gwen wakes up with her own tummy trouble...

TORCHWOOD DECLASSIFIED 2.9 First shown BBC2 13 March 2008
Interviewees: Mike Crowley (special effects supervisor), Russell T Davies, Phil Ford, Nerys Hughes, Eve Myles, Kai Owen, Richard Stokes, Ashley Way

ANALYSIS

Everyone loves a wedding, and Torchwood's take on the big day has all the ingredients for a day to remember – that is until you're retconned, at least. Everything is here, from troublesome in-laws and seriously big hats, to shape-shifting killers and singularity scalpels. It's Torchwood meets Coronation Street, as writer Phil Ford has pointed out.

And where there's soap opera, there's always a strong matriarch or two, and that's the crux of Something Borrowed. The story centres on the maternal instinct, be it Gwen saddled with a very unwelcome pregnancy, her and Rhys' mams bickering over what's best for their offspring, or Carrie the Nostrovite's unstoppable mother love. Rhys even has the Freudian fun of seeing his own mother explode! Well, almost...

Despite all the laughs, the episode rarely lets up on the action, either – from the brutal beginning of Gwen's boozy hen night, to the race against time to get the egg out of her stomach. Unusually for Torchwood, the action mostly takes place away from the city, and like last year's Countrycide (and yet so unlike it!) it makes for a refreshing change of pace in the very heart of the series. There's something strangely satisfying about the team tackling aliens amid flowing dresses and flower arrangements, and Gwen is coolly iconic firing bullets from her bouquet.

Like any good wedding, it's a chance to catch up with the family, and the guest cast are all on winning form. It's also a time for renewing bonds, as Tosh and Owen grow closer after their recent spat, and Ianto dances openly with Jack after weeks of only private moments. But it remains Gwen and Rhys' day most of all – as well as a real treat for the fans. Three cheers for the bride and groom!

FIRST DRAFT

■ Gwen originally overcame the male Nostrovite with help from a discarded umbrella.

■ In the Hub, Tosh and Owen discussed the 1972 Amicus film, Tales From The Crypt.

■ A dream sequence originally saw Gwen transform into the Nostrovite, attacking Rhys in the middle of the wedding ceremony.

■ Jack initially retconned Gwen and Rhys, faking evidence of a perfect wedding. This was altered to emphasise the honesty that underpins their marriage.

CONTINUITY & TRIVIA

■ Gwen's pregnancy cravings kick in straight away, as she wolfs down gherkins during her argument with Jack.

■ Eve Myles' belly prosthetic was designed with an anatomically accurate lower portion, which was cut off, and used by John Barrowman as a soap dish.

■ Both William Thomas, who plays Gwen's dad Geraint, and Nerys Hughes, who plays Rhys' mum Brenda, appeared in Doctor Who in the 1980s.

■ The Singularity Scalpel from Reset is used again, this time modified by Owen to include an LCD screen.

■ The crew blew up an old life cast of Matt Lucas from Little Britain to create the exploding Nostrovite effect at the end of the episode!

■ Tosh shows off her legs, after Henry Parker suggested she do so in the previous episode, A Day In The Death.

■ With the demise of Mervyn, Ianto can be seen taking on DJ duties at the reception.

■ Phil Ford also wrote the two-part stories Eye Of The Gorgon and The Lost Boy for The Sarah Jane Adventures.

2.76m

BARB final rating for 12 March broadcast, in millions

CREDITS & DATES

CREDITED CAST Captain Jack **John Barrowman**, Gwen **Eve Myles**, Owen **Burn Gorman**, Tosh **Naoko Mori**, Ianto **Gareth David-Lloyd**, The Ghost Maker **Julian Bleach**, Pearl **Camilla Power**, Jonathan Penn **Craig Gallivan**, David Penn **Stephen Marzella**, Faith Penn **Hazel Wyn Williams**, Nettie **Lowri Sian Jones**, Christina **Eileen Essell**, Restaurant Owner **Anwen Carlisle**, Senior Nurse **Yasmin Wilde**, A&E Nurse **Caroline Sheen**, Young Dad **Alastair Sill**, Young Mum **Catherine Olding**

WRITER Peter J Hammond
DIRECTOR Jonathan Fox Bassett
PRODUCER Richard Stokes
EXECUTIVE PRODUCERS
Russell T Davies and Julie Gardner

BROADCAST DATES
First shown BBC3 12 March 2008
Repeated BBC2 19 March 2008
Pre-watershed edit first shown
BBC2 20 March 2008

FILMING BLOCK
Five: 13 September-17 October 2008

PLOT SYNOPSIS

Jonathan, a cinema enthusiast, is editing archive footage, when a sinister ringmaster appears unexpectedly on the film. Jonathan tries to cut the film, but a window bursts open and it spools itself back onto the projector.

It's a rainy night and Ianto, Gwen and Owen head to the Electro, a cinema museum where Jonathan works. He arrives with the film, but again the ringmaster appears, along with other circus footage, when the film is played. Ianto spots Jack among the circus acts, before a pair of fleeting shadows pass across the wall behind him. Nearby, a girl is waiting at a bus stop as two oddly dressed figures approach from out of the rain. One of them is the ringmaster from the film. When he touches the girl she becomes cataleptic, and he catches her breath in a flask. Torchwood study the film from the Electro, and see Jack and the 'Night Travellers'. Jack explains he worked with a travelling show for a while, but the Night Travellers were always thought to be a myth. Ianto notices that two of the Night Travellers are now missing from the film. At a derelict lido, the two Night Travellers plan to bring the rest of their company into the modern world, for which they will need the rest of the film.

The pair steal the breath of numerous victims, whom Jack and Ianto visit in hospital. A nurse overhears Jack say "They came from out of the rain," a phrase that used to be associated with the Night Travellers, and says that an elderly patient used to say the same thing. Ianto and Jack visit the old woman, who tells them about the Ghost Maker, who keeps his victims' last breaths in a flask.

Jack says they can save the people in the hospital if they can acquire the flask.

The Ghost Maker takes a film from Jonathan's flat, and plays it at the Electro, allowing the other Night Travellers to emerge. Jack realises they can be stopped if they are captured on film again. He records them and exposes the film to sunlight, causing them to burn away. But as a final vindictive act, the Ghost Maker throws his flask into the air, releasing the breaths within. Ianto catches it in time to save the breath of just one little boy – the only victim they are able to save.

ERM...
As ever, Peter J Hammond leaves many questions unanswered – such as who are the Ghost Maker and Pearl, and where do they come from?

TORCHWOOD DECLASSIFIED 2.10 First shown BBC2 19 March 2008
Interviewees: Jonathan Fox Bassett, Chris Chibnall, Russell T Davies, Marie Doris (makeup artist), Bev Gerard, Peter J Hammond, Ray Holman (costume designer), Camilla Power, Richard Stokes.

ANALYSIS

The power of the past and pictures brought to life are hardly departures for veteran writer Peter J Hammond. He returned to those themes more than once in his fantasy classic Sapphire And Steel, but always with good cause, as they are archetypes of human fear. Throw in a scary circus and the promise of the Torchwood team at the top of their game, and From Out Of The Rain was always going to be a winner.

At its heart, the Ghost Maker and Pearl are fascinatingly creepy creations. At first seemingly creaky and clichéd, it becomes apparent that – beneath their circus personas – they are all too human in their twisted passions and psychopathic tendencies. Whether they are in fact human is never quite explained as, like any good ghost story, the episode thrives on atmosphere and insinuation, rather than hard facts to explain the scares away.

As the two Night Travellers, Julian Bleach and Camilla Power are wonderfully unnerving, taking perverse, sexualised pleasure in their victims, and never quite seeming sympathetic, despite their faded glamour and yearning for a lost age. The similarly forgotten lido where they make their home is the perfect contrast to the gaudy world we see in flashback, and the unusually lingering direction and compelling music give the whole affair an oddly dream-like quality.

But it's not all about the villains, and we get still more development for this series' most fleshed-out character, Ianto, and (as with PJ Hammond's first series episode, Small Worlds), further hints at Jack's diverse experiences during the 20th Century. The interplay between Owen and Gwen at the Electro during a rare night off is also welcome, given how little the two characters' paths have crossed this series.

Still, it's the memory of the Ghost Maker and Pearl that will linger longest about this episode: a pair of truly original creations, albeit it in the classic PJ Hammond mould. The travelling shows may have been forgotten, but these two will be remembered long after the circus has left town.

FIRST DRAFT

■ In the early drafts, The Ghost Maker stole his victims' shadows as well as their last breaths, but the production team thought this was too abstract as a threat, and would be impossible to depict realistically on screen.

■ The Ghost Maker and Pearl originally kept their audience of ghosts/shadows at the Electro, not the lido.

■ Ianto's role was expanded to include some of Gwen's lines, as Eve Myles was filming episode 11, Adrift, at the same time as From Out Of The Rain.

CONTINUITY & TRIVIA

■ Peter J Hammond's fourth Sapphire And Steel adventure from 1981 features figures come to life from photographs.

■ In the circus flashback, the strong man is called Stromboli, in reference to the villainous showman in Disney's 1940 film of Pinocchio, who scared writer Peter J Hammond as a child.

■ The circus scenes were filmed in Cardiff's Bute Park, which also doubled as Hooverville in the 2007 Doctor Who episodes Daleks In Manhattan/Evolution Of The Daleks. However, the Phoenix cinema, which serves as the Electro, is not the same cinema seen in those episodes.

■ Ianto mentions his father again, whom we learned in the last episode was a master tailor.

■ Jack's phrase, "Cinema killed the travelling show," echoes Buggles' 1979 pop hit Video Killed The Radio Star.

■ Jack was presumably sent by Torchwood to investigate the Night Travellers. The following episode, Fragments, suggests Jack freelanced for the Institute throughout the 20th Century.

■ Gerald Carey is credited but does not appear in this episode.

2.90m

BARB final rating for 19 March broadcast, in millions

CREDITS & DATES

CREDITED CAST Captain Jack Harkness **John Barrowman**, Gwen Cooper **Eve Myles**, Owen Harper **Burn Gorman**, Toshiko Sato **Naoko Mori**, Ianto Jones **Gareth David-Lloyd**, Rhys Williams **Kai Owen**, PC Andy Davidson **Tom Price**, Nikki Bevan **Ruth Jones**, Jonah Bevan **Robert Pugh**, Young Jonah **Oliver Ferriman**, Helen **Lorna Gayle**

WRITER Chris Chibnall
DIRECTOR Mark Everest
PRODUCER Richard Stokes
EXECUTIVE PRODUCERS
Russell T Davies and Julie Gardner

BROADCAST DATES
First shown BBC3 19 March 2008
Repeated BBC2 21 March 2008
Pre-watershed edit first shown
BBC2 27 March 2008

FILMING BLOCK
Seven: 18 September–5 October 2008

PLOT SYNOPSIS

When a teenager disappears on his way home from football, Jack shows up on CCTV footage, causing Gwen's former colleague PC Andy to suspect Torchwood are involved. Gwen says she knows nothing about it, but agrees to meet the boy's mother, Nikki, as a fresh eye on the case. Nikki still holds out hope of finding her son, Jonah, and is organising a support group for relatives of other missing persons. Gwen and Andy agree to attend.

In the Hub, Gwen asks Tosh to look for signs of Rift activity on the date that Jonah disappeared. She finds nothing at first, but then detects a negative reading, something Torchwood has always previously overlooked. They realise that the Rift might be taking things from Cardiff, as well as leaving alien things behind.

Jack has denied any knowledge of Jonah's disappearance, saying the CCTV footage is a coincidence, so Gwen asks Tosh to keep their discovery to themselves for now, while she conducts her own investigations.

At the meeting, Gwen is overwhelmed by the number of people who turn up, all with missing loved ones. She cross-references details of the missing people with negative Rift readings and finds an alarming pattern of correspondence. She takes her findings to Jack and the team, but is shocked when Jack warns her off, claiming there is nothing that Torchwood can do.

Taking a break from work, Gwen and Rhys argue about starting a family. Mindful of Nikki's loss, she says it is impossible with the work she does.

Returning to work, Gwen finds a package with coordinates for a tiny nearby island, which she deduces has been left by Ianto.

On the island, Gwen finds an underground hospice full of people taken by the Rift. Jack is there too, and explains that he set the facility up to help them. Gwen sees Jonah, who is now a scarred and haunted middle-aged man.

Gwen tells Nikki she has found Jonah, and she insists on seeing him. They go to the island, where Nikki is shocked by how disturbed her son is after his ordeal. She leaves, making Gwen promise not to tell anyone else the truth about the missing people. Before she knew, she still had hope.

TUNE!
In the cafe, as Gwen resolves to go to Flat Holm island in search of answers, the song Hard To Beat by Hard-Fi plays in the background.

TORCHWOOD DECLASSIFIED 2.11 First shown BBC2 21 March 2008
Interviewees: Chris Chibnall, Russell T Davies, Ruth Jones, Eve Myles, Tom Price, Robert Pugh, Richard Stokes.

Gwen has always been the heart of Torchwood, but hearts can fail, with devastating results. There are no winners in Adrift, as Gwen's emotional ties to her job create tension in her work and home life, and rob a bereft mother of the hope that gives her strength. But Gwen is not negligent or reckless in her quest for the truth; rather it is her own well of hope that convinces her that every problem must have a solution. Like Nikki, with her unexpectedly successful support group, Gwen will always tap into the righteous passion she feels, and harness it for positive action. But while Nikki might find some comfort in the people around her, Gwen becomes more and more isolated as she sails a lonely course – literally adrift amid the slate grey sea and sky.

It's a daring departure for Torchwood to take, putting Gwen into such a morally ambiguous story with so little sci-fi shrouding. The issues addressed are real and raw, and the Rift serves only as the launch pad for a tale of loss and loneliness. Eve Myles is as magnificent as ever (shedding real tears in her big scene with Jonah), and Ruth Jones is the perfect match for her as the similarly determined Nikki.

Inviting sympathy while always staying strong, Nikki evokes all the same qualities as Gwen, but without the resources or knowledge of Torchwood at her disposal. That those resources finally bring nothing but bad feeling is not damning for Gwen or Torchwood: simply a reminder, Spider-Man style, that great power brings with it great responsibility.

The story may belong to Gwen and Nikki, but it serves to highlight the importance of the team dynamic nonetheless. In Chris Chibnall's first episode this series, Kiss Kiss, Bang Bang, we see the team working as a coherent unit, while Fragments explores the stories that bring them together. Here, we see what happens when the heart and the head pull in different directions, rather than complementing each other. Gwen's actions may be rash, but Jack's austere solution is little better. Both do what they can to help, but they always do it best together.

FIRST DRAFT

■ Instead of arguing in the park, Gwen originally made fun of Rhys for his growing admiration for Captain Jack.

■ Ianto's description of Jack as "Innovative, bordering on the avant garde," from Reset was actually written for this episode.

■ Ianto initially slipped Gwen the coordinates for Flat Holm island on a Post-it.

■ Nikki was afforded some solace at the end of the first draft, with the hint of a possible relationship between her and PC Andy.

CONTINUITY & TRIVIA

■ Although the Cardiff Barrage was originally designed to have a public walkway linking Cardiff and Penarth, there is currently no pedestrian route across its span, such as Jonah is using when he disappears.

■ In the Bible, Jonah is a prophet who is swallowed and later spat out by a giant fish.

■ PC Andy refers to Captain Jack as "Mulder", the alien-chasing protagonist in The X-Files.

■ In reality, the cafe seen in the episode has photographs of numerous celebrities on its walls, including John Barrowman...

■ The date of the meeting on Nikki's Searchlight flyer is deliberately obscured, as any mention of specific dates can play havoc with Torchwood and Doctor Who continuity!

■ Gwen was going to adopt Rhys' surname Williams in this episode, but Eve Myles was adamant that her character was an independent woman who would keep the name Cooper.

■ Adrift is series two's 'double banked' episode, filmed at the same time as the two Block Five episodes: From Out Of The Rain and Fragments.

2.52m

BARB final rating for 21 March broadcast, in millions

2.12: FRAGMENTS

CREDITS & DATES

CREDITED CAST Captain Jack **John Barrowman**, Gwen **Eve Myles**, Owen **Burn Gorman**, Tosh **Naoko Mori**, Ianto **Gareth David-Lloyd**, Rhys **Kai Owen**, Weevil/Blowfish **Paul Kasey**, Tosh's Mother **Noriko Aida**, Alice Guppy **Amy Manson**, Emily Holroyd **Heather Craney**, Little Girl **Skye Bennett**, Alex **Julian Lewis Jones**, Bob **Simon Shackleton**, Security Guard **Gareth Jones**, Milton **Clare Clifford**, Katie Russell **Andrea Lowe**, Doctor **Richard Lloyd-King**, Nurse **Catherine Morris**, Psychiatrist **Selva Rasalingham**

WRITER Chris Chibnall
DIRECTOR Jonathan Fox Bassett
PRODUCER Richard Stokes
EXECUTIVE PRODUCERS Russell T Davies and Julie Gardner

BROADCAST DATES
First shown BBC3 21 March 2008
Repeated BBC2 28 March 2008
Pre-watershed edit first shown BBC2 3 April 2008

FILMING BLOCK
Five: 13 September-17 October 2008

PLOT SYNOPSIS

Detecting four aliens lifeforms in an abandoned building, Jack, Tosh, Owen and Ianto split up and find instead four bombs, which explode, trapping them all in the rubble. As it falls to Gwen and Rhys to rescue the team, their lives pre-Torchwood flash before them.

In the 1890s, Jack comes to the attention of the nascent Torchwood. His habits of surviving death and talking about an alien called the Doctor pique their interest, and they offer him his freedom in exchange for his help. Jack spends many years as a freelance field agent for Torchwood, until New Year's Eve 1999, when its latest leader, Alex Hopkins, kills his team, then himself, after glimpsing the 21st Century via an alien device. Alex tells Jack he must take over Torchwood and give it a purpose.

Flash forward four years, and Tosh is living a dull office life by day, and using her genius to build a sonic modulator by night. As she hands the device to a shady gang who are holding her mother hostage, soldiers storm the building. Tosh is held in a military prison, until Jack calls in a favour. He secures her release, and she agrees to work for him.

Unlike Tosh, it is Ianto who tracks Jack down when we see his introduction to Torchwood Three, but Jack will have nothing to do with him. He helps Jack fight a Weevil, and brings him coffee outside the Hub. But it is only when the pair chase and capture a pterodactyl that Jack agrees to give him a chance.

Finally, Owen becomes part of the team after his fiancée Katie, dies as a result of an alien lifeform growing in her brain. Owen sees Jack at the hospital where she dies, but later there is no sign of him on the security CCTV footage. Jack is impressed by Owen's determination to find him, and offers him a job as Torchwood's medic. Broken-hearted and knowing that he can never save enough lives, Owen consents.

Back in the present day, Gwen and Rhys succeed in rescuing the team from the destroyed building. As Gwen asks who was responsible for the trap, a projection of Captain John Hart appears from Jack's wrist strap. John says he has found Jack's long-lost brother Gray, and now he is going to tear Jack's world apart...

ERM...
Did Jack work with Gerald and Harriet (from To The Last Man)? Was he working for Torchwood in Lahore in 1909 (as seen in Small Worlds)?

TORCHWOOD DECLASSIFIED 2.12 First shown BBC2 3 April 2008
Interviewees: John Barrowman, Jonathan Fox Bassett, Chris Chibnall, Gareth David-Lloyd, Russell T Davies, Burn Gorman, Naoko Mori, Richard Stokes

ANALYSIS

Four short stories about Torchwood could have felt slight or self-indulgent, but with its linking theme of how our heroes (minus Gwen, whose own introductory story has already been told) came to join the organisation that shaped them, Fragments enriches the contemporary Torchwood world as much as it expands on what went before.

From the newly deathless Jack, looking for purpose in a life that never ends, to the open and vulnerable Owen who can never save enough people, these are all characters in search of a saving grace to make it everything seem worthwhile. In a show where the physical and emotional toll on its heroes sometimes seems like too much for anyone to bear, it's a timely reminder of how much good comes from what they do – not just in saving the world, but in saving themselves, thanks to Jack and the organisation he rebuilt in a better image.

But if that all sounds a bit too heavy, especially after the harrowing Adrift, Fragments is also a lot of fun. Writer Chris Chibnall's lightness of touch doesn't hammer home his point, but draws it out skilfully amid a feast of diverse set-pieces, from run-away pterodactyl to Blowfish in breeches. The production team goes to town on these, and delights in details such as the Victorian Hub, as seen through a window, and costumes for the regulars that contrast tellingly with our heroes as we know them.

Each one of the segments is totally distinct and would easily stand expansion to an entire episode in its own right, but it is their tantalising concision that truly makes them so appealing. Of course, we all want to know more about these characters and where they came from, but they must also retain some mystery, and room for the imagination to run wild. This is of course most true in the case of Jack, who has a lot more history than most, and it is a pleasure to dip into it at the turning of two centuries, without dwelling too much on just what went on in the years in between. It's a delight, too, to find out that Tosh was once a wanted criminal, of sorts, and that Owen was once driven by pure and simple love for his fiance. Ianto's story is rich with light and shade for the long-term fan, and a straightforward romp for newcomers, but it is the stories of the characters we were about to lose that prove most poignant with hindsight.

FIRST DRAFT

■ Jack's meeting with Tosh was more light-hearted at first. His suggested cover story for her was "Gone round the world hiking with nymphomaniac sextuplets," adding, "We have equipment that'll make your hair curl. That's a metaphor. We don't just have curling tongs."

■ Jack was to be impaled on a steel pole after the explosion, mirroring the broken bottle later seen in his stomach.

■ The end sequence originally saw Captain John reappear with the teenage Gray held captive.

CONTINUITY & TRIVIA

■ A working title for the episode was Blast From The Past.

■ The little girl with the Tarot cards from Dead Man Walking makes another appearance. Like Jack, the girl does not appear to have aged in the 100-plus years that separate the episodes.

■ Another member of the Blowfish species from Kiss Kiss, Bang Bang also appears in the Victorian scenes. In common with his 21st Century counterpart, he is accused of stealing a vehicle – in this case a horse and carriage.

■ In the 1999 Hub scenes, the base of the central sculpture is not shown, as it had not yet been built.

■ Alex's line "21st Century, Jack. Everything's gonna change. And we're not ready." echoes Jack's regular opening monologue.

■ The MOD facility where Tosh worked before joining Torchwood is, in fact, a BBC office building.

■ Tosh's mother was previously seen with a head wound in the series one episode End Of Days.

■ Ianto refers the destruction of Torchwood One, from the 2006 Doctor Who episode The Parting Of The Ways.

2.4m
Overnight ratings for 28 March broadcast, in millions

CREDITS & DATES

CREDITED CAST Captain Jack Harkness **John Barrowman**, Gwen Cooper **Eve Myles**, Owen Harper **Burn Gorman**, Toshiko Sato **Naoko Mori**, Ianto Jones **Gareth David-Lloyd**, Rhys Williams **Kai Owen**, Captain John Hart **James Marsters**, PC Andy **Tom Price**, Gray **Lachlan Nieboer**, Weevil **Paul Kasey**, Dr Angela Connolly **Golda Rosheuvel**, Nira Docherty **Syreeta Kumar**, Charles Gaskell **Cornelius Macarthy**, Alice Guppy **Amy Manson**

WRITER Chris Chibnall
DIRECTOR Ashley Way
PRODUCER Richard Stokes
EXECUTIVE PRODUCERS Russell T Davies and Julie Gardner

BROADCAST DATES
First shown BBC2 4 April 2008
Pre-watershed edit first shown BBC2 10 April 2008

FILMING BLOCK
Six: 21 October–22 November 2008

PLOT SYNOPSIS

The team split up to deal with separate threats around the city, caused by Captain John. Jack finds John in the Hub, where John shoots him and chains him up. The others easily overcome John's diversions, before he tells them to get to the rooftops, to see him lay waste to Cardiff with a series of huge explosions. He then takes Jack away in a Riftstorm.

All of Cardiff's communications are down, and transport routes are cut off. Gwen, Rhys and Andy coordinate the police response, while Owen and Ianto try to limit the chaos elsewhere, and Tosh heads for the Hub.

John has taken Jack back in time to before Cardiff was built. He explains he had to bring Jack back this far to escape the signal that is controlling him. He has not come back far enough, however, as Jack's brother Gray appears, embraces Jack, then stabs him. Driven by hatred for the brother who left him, Gray makes John dig a grave for Jack, burying him beneath what will one day be his adopted city.

In the present day, Gwen finds John in the Hub, and he tells the team to scan for a signal. He says he has been released from Gray's control, and has come back to save Jack, but a scan reveals nothing. Gray has also come to the Hub, using Weevils to attack the city, and trapping Gwen, Ianto and John in their own cells. Tosh reaches the Hub, unaware that Gray is there, and finds that a

TUNE!
John plays Hot Gossip's **I Lost My Heart To A Starship Trooper**, which samples music from Star Wars – a film he also references in Kiss Kiss, Bang Bang.

nearby nuclear power station is going into meltdown. Only a dead man can get past the Weevils, so Owen heads for the facility. Tosh prepares to tell Owen what to do, but Gray shoots her first.

Hearing a noise, Gray finds Jack, revived from stasis in the vaults. The signal John was searching for came from a ring he had buried with Jack, and Torchwood detected it in 1901. They dug Jack up, after 2,000 years buried alive, froze him, and set the alarm for 107 years time. Jack forgives Gray, then chloroforms him.

In agony, Tosh helps Owen save the power station, but a power surge seals him in, where the radiation will destroy his body. Tosh and Owen say goodbye, and shortly after Owen is lost, Tosh also dies in Jack's arms.

Later, Jack puts Gray into stasis, and John leaves, expressing sorrow to Jack for the team's losses.

TORCHWOOD DECLASSIFIED 2.13 First shown BBC2 4 April 2008
Interviewees: John Barrowman, Chris Chibnall, Burn Gorman, James Marsters, Naoko Mori, Eve Myles, Lachlan Nieboer, Richard Stokes, Ashley Way.

ANALYSIS

And so it all comes to a head. Captain John, Gray, Tosh and Owen, the King of the Weevils... Even Rhys and PC Andy get to put aside their differences and fight shoulder to shoulder in this tale of bonds broken and loose ends tied. What could easily have been a retread of episode one, or a kind of greatest hits package, skilfully weaves together the disparate elements set up throughout the series to create something more than the sum of its parts. By the time Victorian Torchwood makes an appearance, it's impossible to know where the story will go next, and the sucker punch that follows hits like the bullet in Tosh's belly.

For an episode that never lets up the pace, the moment when Gray shoots Tosh seems to last an eternity. As the rest of the plot plays out elsewhere, the image of Tosh stays with you insistently, as you will her to survive just a few minutes longer – just long enough for the credits to start to roll...

But it is not to be, and Tosh's final moments are played out with heartbreaking dramatic irony. In life, it seemed as if Owen was always just out of Tosh's reach, no matter how closely the two of them worked together. Now, in death, they spoke intimately through their earpieces, but were further away than ever. That Owen has no idea Tosh is dying during their exchange makes her isolation even more total than his own, sealed inside a coffin of lead.

Both Burn Gorman and Naoko Mori turn in stunning final performances, and Mori in particular encapsulates everything that made Tosh so lovable, as she selflessly puts saving the city, and consoling Owen, ahead of her own mortal plight. The rest of the cast also do justice to their departing co-stars, with some of their most heartfelt moments to date. James Marsters adds layers to his larger than life character, and newcomer Lachlan Nieboer is eerily accurate in his twisted take on John Barrowman's Captain Jack.

By the end of the episode, we are faced with the prospect of a very different Torchwood, where every life-or-death scenario will be be exactly that. Long after they are gone, Tosh and Owen's impact will continue to be felt.

CONTINUITY & TRIVIA

■ The "Central Server Building" in Cardiff is really Stadium House, Wales' tallest building.

■ Golda Rosheuvel reprises her role as Doctor Angela Connolly from Dead Man Walking.

■ The Hoix was first seen in the 2006 Doctor Who episode Love And Monsters.

■ Captain John's line "It's just sex, sex, sex with you people!" is not the same piece of footage that appears in the series two teaser trail at the end of Kiss Kiss, Bang Bang.

■ Emily Holroyd was scripted to appear alongside Alice Guppy in the 1901 scenes, but Heather Craney was not available to reprise her role from Fragments. Instead, Cornelius Macarthy was cast as Charles Gaskell.

■ Jack chloroforms Gray in much the same way as he subdued Owen when they first met in Fragments.

■ Tosh remembers covering for Owen during the "space pig" incident, answering the long standing question of why she was performing a medical exam on the hapless porker in the 2005 Doctor Who episode Aliens Of London.

FIRST DRAFT

■ At first, Captain John was to attack Cardiff with a glowing spherical device that drained all the electricity from the city.

■ The mysterious cowled figures encountered by Tosh and Ianto were originally explained as being harmless projections from a Time Agent device called a Temporal Scavenger.

■ Gwen's rallying of the police force initially countered a rabble-rousing speech by a Sergeant Temple, who advocated a "zero tolerance" approach to the chaos, similar to marshal law.

2.7m
Overnight ratings for 4 April broadcast, in millions

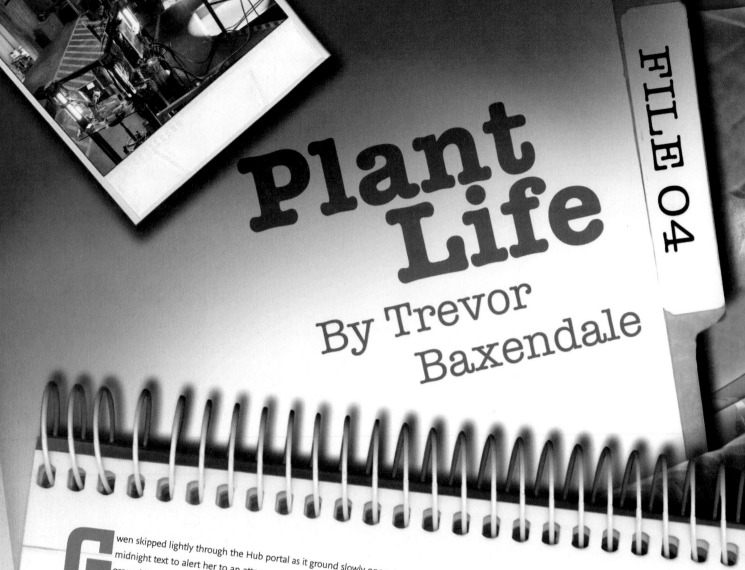

Plant Life

By Trevor Baxendale

Gwen skipped lightly through the Hub portal as it ground slowly open. It wasn't something she did very often. There was usually something to worry about — a midnight text to alert her to an attempted alien invasion or some kind of extra-dimensional incursion through the Rift — and any step taken into the underground headquarters of Torchwood could be a step closer to death.

But not today. Today was different. Today was normal. Properly normal. And nothing was going to stop it being normal.

"Good afternoon," yelled Captain Jack.

Gwen smiled to herself as she jogged up the steps to his office.

He was sitting back with his boots up on the desktop, a wide, gleaming white smile splitting his face in half. "Nice of you to show up for work today, Mrs Williams," he continued. "That's if you actually had doing any work in mind. You could just float around the place looking all love-struck and everything if you'd prefer. It says in the rule book you can do that in lieu of a honeymoon."

"Cooper," said Gwen, still grinning. "I'm keeping my own name. Rhys has agreed."

"Oh, he has, has he?"

"Yeah. Said it wouldn't be me if I wasn't Gwen Cooper anymore. Besides," Gwen raised her left hand and waggled her fingers, "this says I'm a Mrs."

"And what does that say?" Jack pointed a finger at the thing under her left arm.

She looked down as if surprised. "This? It doesn't say anything. It's a plant."

"A plant."

"Yeah. Spider plant. For the flat. I picked it up from the market this morning on the way in. Do you like it?"

She held out the spindly little plant for Jack to see. He straightened up, a slight look of repulsion on his movie star face. "Not keen on spiders."

Gwen laughed, following him out of the office and down towards Tosh's desk space. Toshiko was staring intently at the phalanx of glowing computer screens that constituted her workstation.

"Morning, Gwen," she said without looking up. Reflections of the monitors flickered in her glasses. "How's married life?"

"Fantastic," Gwen told her, gleefully spinning Tosh around in her chair. She skipped after Jack. "I never knew you were scared of spiders."

"I'm not. I said I wasn't keen on them. We had a falling out on Janus Prime, spiders and me."

"Well, this is just a plant, that's all. No worries." Gwen plonked the potted plant down on her desk and bounced into her seat.

Jack frowned. "I hope all this post-nuptial bliss wears off soon. I'll have to have a word with Rhys, get him to start leaving his dirty socks on the floor and toe-nail clippings in the bed."

"Oh, he does that already," sighed Gwen. "Like I said, no worries."

"I'm nauseous."

"I'm in need of coffee." Gwen rapped her desktop. "Where's Ianto? A Monday Morning Special is required."

"Tea boy's in the Hot House," said Owen as he emerged from the depths of the autopsy room.

"Don't call him that," Gwen chided. "What's he doing in there?"

"My turn to water the plants," explained Ianto. He was carefully pouring a plastic cup full of water into the soil of a pot plant, his face a picture of care and concentration. Ianto Jones approached every one of his duties with the same level of precision and commitment, whether it was making a cup of coffee or aiming a stungun at a Weevil.

The Hot House was the team's quiet area, a small place of tranquillity in the often frenetic environment of the Hub. It was warm and secluded, located in an angular glass pod overlooking the rest of the base.

Gwen turned away from her view of Jack and caught a glimpse of Ianto's pinstripe through the foliage. "I thought this was Owen's thing?"

"Well, I imagine he's got other things on his mind right now," Ianto responded, "what with being dead and everything." He straightened up, observing his handiwork with a high achiever's critical eye. "Besides, if it's in the Hub, it's *my* thing."

Gwen walked along the rack of plants, letting her fingers play through the leaves. "These are all alien, then, are they?"

Ianto shrugged. "Some of them are, certainly. Spores or seeds that have drifted in through the Rift. We plant them and see if they grow. Most die. There are some plants in the universe which don't photosynthesise — and they find carbon dioxide poisonous. Others need specially controlled environments," he tapped the glass of a large blue bottle, "and ultraviolet light. Some only thrive in absolute darkness." He knocked on the lid of a large black box. It was completely sealed and impossible to see into. "There's something growing in here, allegedly."

"How can you be sure?"

"We can't. I call it Schrödinger's plant."

Gwen stooped to look at a small purple flower embedded in rich, peaty soil on the next bench. "What's this one called? It's beautiful."

"Nose Biter," Ianto said flatly. "It's carnivorous."

Gwen jerked back as the jagged petals twitched.

"Not all the plants are alien in origin," Ianto continued as if conducting a tour. "Some come through the Rift from the future and the past. This one is from the Silurian era." He indicated a large, bushy fern.

Gwen pulled an appropriately impressed face, although she had no idea what he was talking about. She looked at the specimen that Ianto had been watering so carefully when she came in. "And what about that one?"

"Ah. That's my favourite."

It was rather plain. Just a thin green stalk and a single, rather nondescript leaf. "Riiight," said Gwen.

"It's really come on in the last few days," Ianto explained. "It was practically dead last week. Owen was all for throwing it out, but I believe in giving everyone a chance."

"Everyone?"

"Thing. Every thing."

Gwen straightened up, bored. "It's very nice."

"All it needed was a drop of water. And a bit of patience."

"Lovely." Gwen turned her full-beam smile on Ianto. "Any danger of a coffee this morning?"

Owen didn't sleep anymore and spent most of his time pottering around the Hub. Captain Jack spent all of his time in the Hub; in fact, his sleeping quarters were located beneath his office, accessed via a salvaged submarine hatch set in the floor. Owen used to think it was just eccentric, but now he understood what it felt like to have no life at all outside Torchwood. Or no life at all, full stop.

Nevertheless, no matter how early Owen checked, Jack was always up and washed and dressed before him and ready to greet the day with that big grin. "Morning!" Jack called from his office as Owen stalked up from the cells. He'd been inspecting the Weevil containment locks, just for something to do. He waved at Jack, who signalled back with a cheery flick of *The Times*. Somewhere up above them a pterodactyl flapped lazily around the roof vault.

"Jack! Owen!" Ianto's voice rang out from somewhere above them. Startled, Owen looked up to see Ianto at the top of the spiral staircase leading to the Hot House. He was in his shirtsleeves, but still with a waistcoat and tie — what passed for early morning casual with Ianto.

"Hey, Ianto," Jack yelled. "What gives?"

"New bud! New bud!" he cried, and then darted back into the Hot House.

Owen and Jack found him peering intently at his plant — it had already become Ianto's plant — and pointing. "Look! Just there. It's a new bud. Isn't that fantastic?"

They examined the plant. Sure enough, just by the leaf, there was a tiny, shiny green bulge.

"I wonder where it came from," Jack mused. "How far across the universe and how many centuries it's travelled to get here and survive."

"It's doing well," Owen conceded. "I'd almost given up on it."

"You *had* given up on it," Ianto said.

"Maybe I could run some tests," Owen suggested. "Cross-check the cell patterns with the stuff in the archives. May tell us something."

"There's no need to waste your time on that," Ianto said. "It's here and it's alive. That's all that matters, surely?"

"It's something to do," Owen insisted.

Jack said, "Why don't you check the archives anyway, see if you can find something that fits the description. Ianto can help. It's going to be a quiet day after all. Tosh is off out and I'm tidying up some stuff with UNIT."

But Ianto wasn't listening. He was very gently pouring water into the pot around the base of his plant, watching the soil soaking it up.

Owen shrugged and headed for the exit. "At the double," he sighed.

"Do you think it likes coffee?" Gwen asked.

Ianto shook his head. "I doubt it. Too many toxins. At the moment all it needs is water."

"At the moment?"

"And love and understanding, of course," Ianto added with a smile.

Gwen laughed gently. "You must have green fingers."

"Hi there," said Jack, strolling into the Hot House. "Thought I'd find you here. Everyone wants to know how Ianto's plant is doing."

"There's another leaf coming through," Ianto said proudly.

"Never a dull moment in Torchwood," Jack said.

"It is sort of cute, don't you think?" smiled Gwen.

"That depends," Jack replied, "on how much it takes Ianto away from his normal duties. Such as coffee."

"Good point," Gwen nodded.

"I'll get you coffee in a moment," Ianto assured them. There was a hint of abruptness in his tone that made Gwen and Jack

pull a face at each other.

"I'll get on with my work," Gwen whispered, heading for the door.

"Yeah," said Jack. "Me too."

"Have you thought of a name for it yet?" Toshiko asked, powering her workstation down for the night.

Ianto shook his head. "No pet names."

"It seems silly not calling it anything," Tosh insisted gently. "We ought to give it a name."

"Owen's been checking through the botanical archives to see if he can find a match," Ianto said, yawning. "We'll know what it is if he finds one."

"You look tired."

Ianto stretched, leaning back on the old settee. "I could do with some sleep, that's true."

"You're spending all your time here," Tosh said. "Nothing unusual there, I know. But you look bushed. Jack won't thank you for being too tired to work. It may be quiet now, but you know how it is around here. Anything could happen at any time. We need to be ready."

Ianto dragged his hands down his face. "I know, I know. I'll go home soon. I'll just check on the plant first." He heaved himself up and headed for the Hot House.

Toshiko watched him mount the staircase, chewing thoughtfully on the arm of her glasses.

"Well, I don't really see any harm in it," Gwen said the next day. They were in the boardroom, Jack playing thoughtfully with a pencil, Gwen sitting on the desk, Tosh next to her. Owen was leaning against the double doors.

the meeting was over. "Okay, back to work, people. I'm getting paranoid in my old age. Scat."

They filed out, but he called Gwen back just before she left. "How did Rhys like the spider plant?" he asked.

She laughed. "Never even noticed it."

The plant was looking very healthy. It was a good couple of centimetres taller, and possibly straighter, with two full leaves and the start of a new one. It still wasn't all that big, or even very special looking, but it now dominated the Hot House.

This was largely due to the fact that nearly all the other plants had gone.

Ianto had moved them out of the Hot House one by one. They were stacked on the steps of the spiral staircase and Toshiko had to climb very carefully through the foliage to reach the door to the pod. Inside, more plants had been moved to the floor on the far side, away from Ianto's own little flower, and many of the racks had been completely cleared.

"Ianto... what's happened up here?"

"Nothing," Ianto grunted, straightening up after placing the heavy glass bell jar containing who-knew-what by the door. "I'm just making a bit of space."

"For what?"

"For the plant. It's getting crowded. It can't grow properly without light and space."

Toshiko stepped into the Hot House, which now seemed very bare. Her voice echoed slightly against the glass walls as she spoke. "Does Owen know you've done this?"

"Owen?" Ianto repeated. "What's it got to do with him?"

"Well, he sort of... kept this place going, didn't he?"

"Owen's got other things on his mind right now. As I think I have already pointed out."

"And you?"

"What about me?"

"Jack says you're obsessed with this plant thing," Toshiko said carefully.

Ianto smiled. "He's just jealous."

"Possibly. You are giving it a lot of attention, though. And it is just a plant, after all."

"He worries too much, and so do you. That's your problem, Tosh. Too much worrying. Sometimes you've just got to do what's right and ignore everything else."

Toshiko was a little taken aback. She had never heard Ianto speak like this. He didn't sound hostile, but there was something wrong. She took a deep breath and said, "I thought it was time we took a sample for investigation."

He looked at her, and saw she was holding a microscope slide.

"You can't," he said.

"I only need a tiny piece," Toshiko said. "I just want to have a look at its cellular make-up."

"You can't," Ianto repeated.

He said it simply, and with a smile, but Toshiko didn't doubt him for a second. "All right," she relented. "But I'll have to tell Jack. He asked specifically. At the very least the plant needs to be catalogued, and we can't do that without a cell sample."

She left the Hot House, still holding the empty slide, while Ianto carefully added a few more drops of water to the plant's soil.

"You think it's a hobby?" Jack asked, unimpressed.

"Well, I don't know much about hobbies."

"Hobbies are for men," Owen commented.

"Ianto doesn't have any hobbies," Jack said.

"He's very fond of that old stopwatch," Gwen said, her eyes full of innocence.

"That's not a hobby," Jack insisted.

"It's only a plant," Toshiko ventured. "What harm can there be?"

"He's obsessed with the thing," Jack said, his voice hardening.

"The plant isn't poisonous, carnivorous, mobile or intelligent," Toshiko continued. "It is, to all intents and purposes, just a plant. I repeat: what harm can there be?"

Jack swivelled around to face Owen. "Have you come up with anything on the database?"

"Nothing. The Torchwood botanical records go back over 100 years. There's nothing on the computer, the microfiche, the ledgers or diaries that fits the description. We don't know what it is. We don't even know," he added meaningfully, "if it's alien."

"What do you mean?" asked Gwen. "I thought all the plants in the Hot House were extraterrestrial in origin, or at least from another time zone."

"So we think," Owen replied. "What proof do we have in this particular case? I should point out that there's nothing that fits the description of the plant in any Earth records either, but I've only been looking for three days and it's a big job."

"We could take a cell sample," Toshiko said. "Put it under the microscope."

"Frankly, I'm surprised you haven't done that already," Jack cut in.

Toshiko looked momentarily fazed, unused to be reprimanded, even mildly. Jack had spoken softly, but he wasn't smiling. "I — I just didn't think it was necessary," she said. "We've been busy with other things. I don't see what the problem is — Ianto's looking after his plant, that's all."

"She's got a point, Jack," Gwen agreed.

Jack sighed and threw his pencil down on the table top, signalling that

"Hey," said Jack from the doorway. "Need a break?"

"No thanks. I'm good here."

"Kinda weird, though," Jack said, leaning against the glass that overlooked the rest of the Hub. He took a sip from his mug of coffee. "I mean, you sitting there like that. Doing nothing."

"I'm not doing nothing," Ianto stated. He didn't look at Jack. His attention was fixed on the plant. It was all that was left in the Hot House now, with the exception of the swivel chair Ianto was sitting on, right in front of it.

"Right," Jack nodded slowly. "I guess I missed that."

"Yes," agreed Ianto. "I guess you did."

"The others are getting pretty worried about you."

"There's no need for anyone to worry. We're fine."

"We?"

"I'm fine. I'm fine, really." Ianto looked up at Jack. "Really."

"Okay," Jack said. He sipped his coffee again and grimaced. "Thing is, we're all drinking lousy coffee here now. This stuff is disgusting. Tastes like Sontaran dysentery. And believe me, that's something you don't want to taste twice."

"There's more to life than coffee."

"What, really?"

"That's all you think I'm good for, isn't it, Jack? Making coffee."

Jack grinned. "Well, I can think of a couple of other things you're good for."

"That's not what I meant and you know it."

Jack moved further into the room, keeping his hands in his pockets, casual. "Ianto, this has gone far enough. You need a break. You haven't slept in two days. You haven't shaved either. And you know what I think of beard rash."

"Bring me a razor and I'll shave."

"Sure. How about a change of clothes too? Because frankly, Ianto, you ain't as fragrant as you used to be."

"I'm not leaving. More important things to do here."

"Just for ten minutes, then. A comfort break?"

"Don't need one. Haven't drunk anything in the last twenty-four hours."

Something crunched under Jack's boot and he noticed some tiny pieces of broken glass glinting on the floor behind Ianto's chair. He stepped carefully over them and leaned on the back of the chair. It creaked slightly but Ianto didn't move. Jack took a deep breath. "Don't you think this is all a little bit... unusual?" Receiving no reply, Jack squatted down at the side of the chair, speaking softly. "Ianto... I need a cell sample from the plant. We have to check it out, see what makes it tick. I mean, we know it doesn't actually tick. We just want to find out what it is, what it's doing."

"It's growing. It's a plant. What else would it do?"

"Well, we don't know. That's why we'd like to check it out." Jack held up a slim rectangle of glass. "I've got a slide right here. Let me take a sample and I can get out of here, leave you and the plant alone together. How does that sound?"

No answer.

"Toshiko's got the equipment ready to go. All she needs is a sample. How about it?"

Still no answer.

Jack moved towards the plant, extending his hand with the microscope slide. Ianto grabbed Jack's wrist, fast as a rattlesnake. His knuckles were white, but his eyes were red — bloodshot, but wide and alert.

"Don't touch it," he hissed. "You can't touch it!"

Jack tried to pull away, but Ianto held him in a surprisingly strong grip. They struggled against each other for a few seconds until Jack wrenched his arm free. "Goddammit, Ianto, I'm not fighting you over a plant!"

"Then don't fight me!" Ianto cried hotly. "Just leave me alone and everything will be fine. Can't you see that?"

Jack stood up, breathing hard. "What's up with your arm?"

"What?" Ianto looked down at his arm, where the shirt cuff had been pulled away to reveal a series of sticking plasters on the white flesh. "Nothing. I had an accident, that's all. I was moving one of the specimens and the jar broke. Cut my arm. It's nothing."

Jack glanced down at the fragments of glass on the floor. "You need to be more careful."

"I'll brush it up later."

"I wasn't talking about the glass."

Jack tossed the slide down onto the floor and walked out.

There was no natural light in the Hub. The Torchwood base was located deep below ground, and there were no windows. It was sometimes impossible to tell the difference between day and night, and this made it very easy to lose track of time. To counteract this, and maintain some vague kind of biological clock, Jack found it useful to dim the lights in the evening, and then turn them right back up in the morning. Ianto had once likened it to life on a submarine. Jack had winked, and told him that he'd once spent many weeks onboard a German U-Boat in World War Two. "Technically I was a prisoner of war, but we were submerged for a long time and, well, sailors are sailors the world over."

That had been in the early days, when Ianto blushed easily. "They're called submariners," he'd muttered. "Not sailors."

Jack smiled at the memory. There was always a hint of the pedant about Ianto. Underneath that soft exterior, there was steel. Very few people got to know that. Those that did usually regretted it.

"He'll be okay," Gwen said quietly, joining him by the circular window in his office which overlooked the Hub. It was gone midnight and the vast chamber was in semi-darkness. On the far side they could see the glow of the lights in the Hot House, and Ianto, still sitting there watching his plant. "We'll find a way."

"Sure. We could just storm in and drag him out if we wanted to," Jack sighed. "That's what Owen wants."

"Since when did you take any notice of what Owen wants?"

"There has to be a better way, Gwen. I don't want him hurt."

"He'll fall asleep eventually. He has to. That's what the police do in siege situations. Wait long enough, and they'll just... nod off."

"Ianto won't. He's tougher than he looks. And that plant's got a grip on him. I don't know how, but I'm going to break that grip, Gwen. That I promise."

"He's moving," Gwen said suddenly.

Ianto was little more than a silhouette, but he had got up from his chair.

They both ran out of the office, Jack leaping down the steps to the lower level while Gwen clattered along behind him. Eventually she managed to grab his arm and pull him to a halt. "Wait!" she hissed. "Don't rush! He'll hear us!"

Owen emerged from the cells, looked at Jack and Gwen, glanced up at the Hot House. He realised immediately something was up and shot a questioning look back at Gwen.

She raised a finger to her lips, signalling caution.

Jack was already moving up the spiral staircase, as quick and silent as a jungle cat. Gwen followed, trying to match him. Automatically, she reached behind her hip for her pistol, only then remembering that it was on her desk. She glanced behind her, past Owen, and saw Tosh heading towards them as well, pausing only to collect her PDA.

In the Hot House, Ianto was bent over his plant. His shirtsleeve was rolled up past his elbow, and his forearm was extended. The plasters had been removed. There were deep cuts in the flesh, and the blood stood out stark and red against the white skin, running down his wrist. His fist was clenched so that the blood came freely, trickling into the soil of the plant pot.

Jack stood in the doorway, transfixed by the sight. He felt as if he was intruding on an intensely private communion. Ianto was oblivious, his full concentration on the plant. As Jack watched, a thin proboscis emerged from the plant stem, extending like the tongue of a hummingbird towards Ianto's arm. It burrowed into the wound, pulsing slightly as it lapped up the blood.

"Bastard!" Jack had seen more than enough, he hurling himself across the room, wrenching Ianto away from the plant. Blood jetted into the air as he spun away, collapsing into the waiting arms of Owen and Gwen. They lowered him gently to the floor.

The plant actually hissed.

Jack swept it off the shelf with enough force to send it crashing into the far wall. The pot burst against the glass in a shower of dirt. The plant hit the floor, white roots writhing in the air, groping like a hundred fingers for the scattered soil. Two quick strides took Jack to where it lay. He raised his boot and crushed the plant flat, screwing his heel down until it left a smear of green and red across the floor.

Instantly, Ianto fell slack. His head lolled as Gwen tried to sit him up. Owen was already putting a field dressing on his arm. "Okay, Ianto, you're all right. We've got you. You're going to be fine..."

Toshiko scanned the remains of the plant with her PDA. "No life signs," she reported. "Whatever it was, it's dead. And not before time, I have to say."

Jack's lip curled in disgust. "What the hell was it?"

"A plant," Owen said. "Some kind of telepathic species, perhaps, using mind control of the local fauna for protection. It used Ianto to look after it, protect it, feed it. He was nothing more than a slave."

"He's all right now, though," Gwen assured him. "The moment you killed it, I felt him relax, like a puppet with its strings cut. He's free of the influence."

Jack turned to leave. "Get this place cleaned up. Get Ianto cleaned up. This room feels dirty now."

Gwen rested a hand on his arm. "Don't be hard on yourself. No one knew what to do for the best."

"Except the plant?"

"It's gone. We're still here. Ianto's still here."

"What if we hadn't been alert? What if it had reproduced, spread seeds, got out of the Hub? Imagine a whole planet with those things growing in every park and hedgerow. The human race could have been reduced to mindless slaves doing nothing but feeding blood-sucking plants." He shrugged, then looked back up at his people. "This is our life, guys. This is Torchwood. We can't relax. We can't hesitate. We have to be ready."

AGING AGYEMAN

FREEMA AGYEMAN UNDERWENT A DRAMATIC TRANSFORMATION IN EPISODE SEVEN, DEAD MAN WALKING. HERE, **ROB MAYOR** FROM MILLENNIUM FX TAKES US BEHIND THE SCENES ON THE COMPLEX PROCEDURE.

2 In the makeup chair, Freema's skin is cleansed and toned to help the adhesives grip for longer. Then prosthetic makeup artists Sarah Lockwood and Charlie Bluett apply a latex-based 'old-age stipple' around Freema's eyes and mouth. "This creates fine and natural-looking wrinkles when it is dried and powdered with talc," says Rob.

1 Weeks before she arrived on the Torchwood set, Freema Agyeman travelled to the Buckinghamshire base of Millennium FX, where she sat for a life cast of her face and neck. "Neill Gorton sculpted the prosthetic over the life cast," says Rob, "which was also used in transit, to help the prosthetic keep its shape."

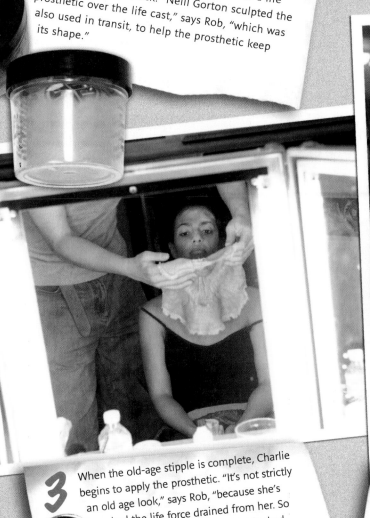

3 When the old-age stipple is complete, Charlie begins to apply the prosthetic. "It's not strictly an old age look," says Rob, "because she's had the life force drained from her. So we went for something that looked quite emaciated and drained, rather than just making her look like a nice, healthy old lady."

4 Because the appliance is so soft and stretchy, just like real skin, both Sarah and Charlie must hold it in place before it is tacked down. "We cast it in two pieces, both made from a material called plat gel," says Rob. "It's a soft, translucent silicone, which we use for all sorts of skin effects."

5 As soon as the lower part of the prosthetic is positioned just right, it is glued in place. The 'flashing' that protects the delicate edges is then carefully removed with scissors, before the edges themselves are all glued down. "Freema had to stay very still throughout the application," says Rob. "But she was great to work with, and extremely patient."

6 The second part of the appliance goes over Freema's forehead, and overlaps the lower piece. It is fixed in place in just the same way, and trimmed to fit around her hairline. "Note the detail in the eyebrows," says Rob. "They had to be punched into the plat gel, one hair at a time!"

7 When the face pieces are both glued down, Charlie sets to work on Freema's hands. "There was no need to extend the appliance to her arms and shoulders," says Rob, "because we arranged with the costume department that Martha would be wearing a long-sleeved top, saving valuable time on the day."

8 At the same time, Sarah double-checks that all the edges are securely glued down and blended in, to withstand the rigours of a long day on set. "By this point, applying the prosthetic has taken about two-and-a-half hours, and it has to be durable enough and comfortable enough that it could be worn all day," says Rob.

WRINKLED, WRINKLED' LITTLE STAR

FREEMA AGYEMAN SHARES SOME OLD AGE WISDOM…

9 When the prosthetic is fully applied, it is art-worked to match Freema's skin tone. Then makeup artist Andrea Dowdall adds the final touch, by working wispy white strands into Freema's hair. "We thought about using contact lenses, too," says Rob. "But it looks even better to see Martha's eyes looking out from this old face."

How did it feel, being turned old for Torchwood?

"I was really glad I got the opportunity to do that. I'd been a bit jealous when David [Tennant] got to have his face done for Doctor Who [in The Sound Of Drums/Last Of The Time Lords], so I thought "Finally, I get to go and play with prosthetics, too!' But now I've done it, I won't be standing at the front of the queue again. It's not as much fun as it looks!"

What was the application process like?

"The first time you have it done, it's really quite scary, because the stuff they put on you sets really quickly, and it feels really tight on your skin. You can't see or hear anything, and you feel like you're being cocooned, so I thought I was going to freak out. But the two guys from Millennium FX are there, saying, "You're doing really well! Keep calm!" So you know it's going to be alright."

Did things get easier when you got on set?

"Once it was on, it was okay for about a couple of hours, but after that you feel itchy and sweaty and you really want to scratch your face. I had to wear it three times: once for just one scene, which was fine; once for about half a day; and once for the whole day, which was pretty difficult. But once I got over the fear the first time, I found it really interesting to watch them applying it, and I loved watching them work."

10 Once on set, the prosthetic is complemented by sympathetic lighting so it will stand up to scrutiny, even close up in High Definition (HD), the format in which Torchwood is filmed. "Bad lighting can ruin weeks of work on a complex prosthetic," laughs Rob. "Luckily, that's not something we've ever had to worry about on Torchwood, though!"

So you were glad to take it off?

"Yes, except that taking it off was probably the worst thing! It's such a messy process and it takes about an hour and a half. There's glue and gunk all over the place and bits of stuff in your hair. I've got so much respect now for people like [Weevil and Blowfish actor] Paul Kasey, who has to go through that all the time. I think it looked fantastic in the end, but once was enough for me!"

In the same episode, you also wrestle with a glove…

"Everyone was chuckling at me when we did that! There were three different gloves: one which was animatronic, one which had a real hand inside it, and one which was made of foam, with a mouthpiece sticking out, so I could hold it between my teeth. I looked absurd, and I could hear everyone chuckling, but all I could say back was, 'Gnnnn? Gfnghh!' It was totally barking. But as soon as you hear 'action' and everyone else is screaming and running around, then you just have to go for it!"

HELÔ!

CARDIFF · NO 1   MARCH 2008

GWEN & RHYS INVITE YOU TO THE

WEDDING OF THE CENTURY

PREMIERE

CAPTAIN JACK HARKNESS AND HIS
DELIGHTFUL DATE TOSHIKO SATO

ALL THE BEHIND THE SCENES DRAMA
WHO IS THIS MYSTERIOUS LADY?

0 123456 789005   01

FOREVER HOLD YOUR RHYS

IT'S THE DAY OF GWEN AND RHYS' WEDDING SO SIT BACK AND ENJOY OUR ON-SET REPORT ON THE BIG DAY…

THERE'S NOTHING LIKE A WEDDING for bringing people together, and today the gang's all here. Thanks to modern editing techniques, it's not unusual for a group of actors to film their various parts of a scene separately, but on this cold, clear day in November, Jack, Owen, Tosh, Ianto – and even Nerys Hughes – have all turned out for Gwen and Rhys' big day.

The venue is Margam Park, near Port Talbot, where a dignified 18th Century Orangery stands amid formal gardens in the shadow of Margam Castle. The Orangery regularly hosts real weddings, but it is just one of several locations serving as Gwen and Rhys' dream destination. Inside, the venue is dressed simply, but elegantly, not unlike Eve Myles herself, who, in a figure-hugging wedding dress, is finally free of the prosthetic belly

"IT'S IMPOSSIBLE NOT TO GRIN WHEN THE COUPLE EXCHANGE VOWS."

👁 SPOTTED!

Torchwood costume designer **Ray Holman** had an experience not dissimilar to Ianto's when he took a tour round Cardiff's bridal shops. "When I asked if they sold maternity wedding dresses, the response was a very firm 'No!' and a look as if I was the biggest sinner in the world!" he says, "especially when I told them we needed three! In the end I had to make them myself. You can get them on the internet, but they're absolutely horrible!"

she has been wearing for most of the episode as the suddenly pregnant Gwen.

"I miss my belly!" she laughs, when Hello! – sorry, Torchwood magazine – ventures that she is looking really good. "You look lovely, too," she lies, as we scuttle away in jeans and T-shirt to join the crew (who are similarly under-dressed) behind a glass partition that divides the room.

Back here is where the reception scenes will take place later on. For now, it's a mass of monitors, makeup bags, cables and crew. Looking out from here into the main area, the only giveaway that this wedding is anything out of the ordinary is the dirty great set of camera tracks cutting across the red carpet, and the professional camera rig that is rolling along it. That's probably de rigueur at all the best weddings nowadays, anyhow.

As the smartly dressed extras who make up the guests file in at the far end of the room, they are more respectful of the red carpet, stepping over it, rather than on it, to reach their seats. When they get there, each one will find a full order of service printed

THE BRIDE EVE MYLES

out (see below), a small part of the realism upon which the Torchwood art department insists. "FOR THE MARRIAGE OF RHYS ALUN WILLIAMS & GWEN ELIZABETH COOPER" it reads. "GWESTY RHYD-YR-AUR FUNCTION SUITE, 1.30PM"

Once the guests are assembled, director Ashley Way must decide whereabouts he wants them all. "It's a lot of people for Torchwood," he says. "I don't think we've done anything this big in terms of people before, but it is a full-on romp, so it's got to have that sense of scale about it.

"It's the second time I've married Eve Myles, actually," he goes on. "I took her up the aisle in an episode of [BBC Wales drama] Belonging a couple of series ago. She wasn't heavily pregnant with an alien in that, though, so this makes for a bit of variety!"

Before this latest wedding can go ahead, Ashley must block out the scene with the bride and groom. Eve chews gum as she mimes kissing Kai Owen (Rhys), and the pair giggle as they go through their lines one more time. Before long, it's time to go for a take, and Ashley moves back behind the partition as the main cast and guest stars take their seats among the guests.

It's impossible not to grin when the couple finally exchange vows. Eve certainly can't help it. And when the congregation applauds, it's hard not to join in, even on the fifth take (which isn't because anyone gets their vows wrong, either – it's just the need for multiple angles). Only Liz Taylor has said her vows more, but each time is still a wonderful, warm and fuzzy moment.

Then it's over, and everyone piles into the reception room to relax for a few minutes. Eve adds a fetchingly cute but incongruous pink

Congratulations Eve! Are you missing your baby bump today?
"You would never believe how weird that bump is! You have to slide into it, like a boob tube, and it looks and feels so realistic, with veins and translucent skin. When it first came back [from Millennium FX] it even had a... 'lady purse' on the bottom of it! Obviously, you're not going to be seeing that, so they cut it off, but somehow John Barrowman heard about it, and next thing I knew he was using it as a soap dish!"

Does it change the way you perform?
"It does and it's very odd! It's weighted to make my posture more realistic, and after about an hour of wearing it, it really feels like a part of me. I keep rubbing it and saying, 'Oh, my back! Can you help me get up?' Then thinking, what am I doing? It's brilliant how it changes the way you move, and how other people react to you. I don't think they know they're doing it, but everyone comes up to touch you!"

Did you ever stick a cushion up your top when you were a kid?
"I'm 29 and I still prance around with tea towels up my top, going, 'What would I look like if I was pregnant?' And now I've seen it almost for real. The first time I put it on, I sent a picture of it to my partner, and he was just gobsmacked! But then, I was in a wedding dress with another man on my arm, so it was a bit of a double whammy for him, really!"

It's a strange way to earn a living, isn't it?
"It is a very odd thing to do for work, yes! Sometimes, poor Kai has to come down from London, just to spend an hour in bed with me, then get back on a train and go all the way back again! What kind of bizarre job is that? If I was him, I'd say 'Tell her to get into bed on her own!' But I do love the bump, and I miss it when I haven't got it on. We're going to call her Nostroviolet!"

R&G

Bridal March
'Lohengrin' – Wagner

Address by Registrar Safiya Wilson

Reading
'Love Times Two'
Read by Melanie Cooper

Love between two cannot be measured.
It is all and everything,
And knows no bounds.
It presides in hearts and sights and sounds.

Love when true can not be broken.
It is strong and pure,
And free and open,
It grows each day and goes unspoken.

Love times one is bliss indeed,
But in truth is left wanting,
Of another love,
A love times two,
Where two loves fuse and are love anew.

And so true love, seen here today,
In two very special hearts,
Can, in no way, be compared,
To love times one when love's declared,
And the joy of two loves paired.

R&G

Reading
'A Wedding Day Rhapsody'
Read by Malcolm Williams

The Marriage Vows

Exchanging of the Rings

The Signing of the Register

'All You Need is Love'
by The Beatles

Wedding March
Mendelssohn

THE GROOM KAI OWEN

Congratulations Kai! How does it feel to be getting married?
"Great! It's a stereotypical Welsh wedding really, isn't it? The bride's pregnant, and there's fighting and bloodshed! When you put Torchwood on top of all that, it's a pretty explosive mix!"

Are you married in real life?
"I'm engaged. But hopefully when we get married I won't have to go at my mam with a chainsaw!"

Is it strange to be going through that ceremony with someone other than your fiancé?
"It is a little bit bonkers, yeah! To be standing at the altar saying those words, with Eve looking gorgeous in her wedding dress, and me in my morning suit, there is a moment when you go, 'Whoah, this is strange!' But at the same time, there's a shapeshifting alien sitting behind us, so it doesn't seem too real!"

What's it like to have Nerys Hughes playing your mum?
"Oh, it's unbelievable, isn't it? I remember seeing her in The District Nurse when I was a little'un! She's absolutely bonkers and she was a star from day one. But Gwen's parents, Will Thomas and Sharon Morgan, and Robin Griffiths, who plays my dad, are all fantastic Welsh actors, too. It's a really good old-fashioned Welsh cast who know what it's all about, and I'm very proud to be working with them."

Is it good to have some action scenes at last?
"Oh yeah, it's such good fun. This is a real belter of an episode, and not just for Rhys. I love doing all the domestic stuff, but it's opened so many doors now he knows about the crazy world of Torchwood. If Gwen says she's pregnant by an alien, that's totally believable to him. It makes it a really good laugh, but you've still got to play it straight, because it's such a ridiculous idea!"

dressing gown to her ensemble, and any vestige of solemnity to the scene is dispelled as she wrestles Burn Gorman into a flower arrangement. John Barrowman offers his input by letting out a huge comedy fart, and makeup designer Marie Doris pursues him with a can of air freshener, vigorously purifying the room.

Soon after comes lunch, and everyone leaves the Orangery in the direction of the car park, where a mobile canteen dishes out meals to be eaten on a converted double-decker bus. To anyone passing the queue of supporting artists all in their Sunday best, it must look like the cheapest wedding reception in history. By now, Eve has changed into a more luxurious, white dressing gown, and is fixing herself a drink at the refreshments table.

"Not very glamorous for a wedding, is it?" she smiles as she looks round the enclosure of trailers. "Forget the champagne! Cup of tea and a kip, that's what I need now." Nerys Hughes, also clad in a bath robe, makes a beeline for us across the car park – a sentence that we never expected to write. "What are you writing?" she

demands. "A Torchwood magazine? How exciting! You must only say nice things!" And, with that, she is gone.

Beyond the trailers are the ruins of Margam Abbey, where some of the crew kick a football around, and others sneak a cigarette before shooting resumes. From here, the scale and grandeur of the Orangery is apparent. It is Grade One listed as one of Wales' finest classical buildings, but tomorrow Torchwood plans to take a chunk out of it.

"We've got permission to remove one of the windows for the stunt where Carrie the Nostrovite smashes through the glass," says Ashley. That'll be one of the floor-to-ceiling Grade One listed 18th Century windows, then? "Yes, one of those. We've got glaziers who will remove it very carefully, replace it with stunt glass, then put it back again at the end of the day." What if it breaks? "We don't want to think about that!" he says. "It would be like the chandelier scene in Only Fools And Horses, wouldn't it? And you wouldn't see us for dust!"

(As it happens, removing the real window proved trickier than expected, and it was

THE WEDDING CRASHER
COLETTE BROWN

SHE FACED VAMPIRES IN ULTRAVIOLET, BUT NOW SHE'S BRINGING HER OWN BITE TO BEAR, AS CARRIE THE MAN-HUNGRY NOSTROVITE!

Hi Colette. Are you getting your teeth into the role of Carrie?
"I'm loving every minute of it, from the flirting to the biting! It does feel like a very complete character, even though she's really a monster. Normally I play quite timid, weak-willed women, and here I am eating people and looking hideous! It's great!"

So what makes her more than just a monster?
"She's not just out to kill: she wants her child back, by any means necessary. I've got children myself, so I know that mothering instinct. And if someone hurts my boy or girl, then mummy will go on the rampage!"

Are you getting into the scary Nostrovite look?
"Oh, yeah! I loved seeing all the prosthetics when I was working on Holby City, and I was always impressed by how real they looked, even when you saw them close up. So, to have it on myself is really great fun! The first time I put it on, I didn't remember to get into costume first, so afterwards they had to dress me, to stop me from putting a claw through my tights or something. It was so funny. I was completely incapable!"

Well, you have to look good for a wedding, don't you...
"Absolutely! And because it's a wedding, I get to see all sorts of beautiful locations around Cardiff, too! I'm a tiny bit disappointed not to have any scenes in the Hub, because I'm told it looks absolutely amazing when you actually get inside. But I've seen some breathtaking places over the course of the shoot, so I really can't complain!"

Presumably you won't be doing the jumping-through-the-window stunt yourself?
"Absolutely not! I'm so in awe of what those stunt guys do. Even a punch has to be done just right not to be dangerous. On [1990s vampire thriller] Ultraviolet, there was a scene where I had to slap Jack Davenport, and he told me to really go for it. So I did, and I think it was harder than he was expecting! He said to the director, 'I hope you got that, because it really hurt!' So you really have to be careful!"

No urges to slap anyone on Torchwood, though?
"No! Everyone's been really welcoming. We're right at the end of the series now, so they're all really tired, but no one's been cranky at all. I've been on sets where everyone's moaning from the start of day one, but here they just say, 'We're tired, but let's go!' and I think that really shows on screen."

Were you a fan of the first series, then?
"Oh, definitely. I think both Torchwood and Doctor Who really are the very best of British, and can match anything that they do in America. I can't tell you how excited I was when they asked me to do this! Other actors might want to appear at the National Theatre, but I was just desperate for a chance to do Torchwood!"

You've done science fiction before, of course...
"I was in Ultraviolet, yes, which still remains one of my favourite jobs to date. Joe Ahearne, who wrote and directed it [and who went on to direct for Doctor Who in 2005], had such a wonderful idea and did a really grand job on it, I think. It was really stylish, in much the same way as Torchwood is now, in fact."

Are you a fan of sci-fi shows in general?
"I really loved Star Trek when I was a kid. My mum is black, and at the time I really thought that she looked like Lieutenant Uhura! So, whenever it came on the television, my dad would always say, 'Look, there's mum!' and for ages and ages he totally convinced me that it was her!"

Wedding crasher, window smasher: Colette Brown's stunt double makes short work of the tall window, originally intended to replace some of the Orangery's real glass.

"NAOKO MORI PICKS UP HER HANDBAG AND A GUN THAT'S NOT MUCH SMALLER."

THE MONSTER-IN-LAW
NERYS HUGHES

THE STAR OF THE LIVER BIRDS AND THE DISTRICT NURSE IS
EQUALLY FEARSOME AS BATTLEAXE BRENDA OR MURDEROUS MONSTER!

Hello Nerys. Are you feeling motherly?
"I'm a grandmother, never mind a mother! I can't pretend I'm younger than I am, because everyone knew me in the 1970s, when I did The Liver Birds, and they've watched me grow up in the 80s and 90s. But I hope my spirit's still young!

Is it good to be back in Wales?
"It's lovely! I did [1980s period drama] The District Nurse here for about six years, and the Torchwood cast have all made me feel at home again straight away. It's marvellous to see Wales back on the map. We're so bloody trendy now thanks to things like this! I'm chuffed they asked me to be in it. And the best thing is that I get to be a monster!"

Is that a new experience for you?
"Well, I've played all kinds of weirdos on stage, but never a monster! For this, I have fangs and claws and red eyes, and I get to be wired up so all this

black blood can ooze out when I get shot! It's so much fun, and the lovely director [Ashley Way] has already told me to calm down a bit! I'm Welsh, so I do tend to throw myself into things!"

So you're having a good time?
"Oh, it's lovely. They're a very warm group, and everyone has really done their best to involve me. Kai Owen is so sweet and funny, and I really rate Eve Myles. I did a comedy pilot with her about five years ago, and she made everyone go 'wow!' She's not just stunning to look at, she's also got this lovely, radiant warmth about her."

It's not your first brush with sci-fi, is it?
"No, it's not. I was in Doctor Who about 25 years ago [1982's Kinda], so I do feel like I'm a part of the family. I never quite understood the story, but we all did it with absolute sincerity. You've got to do it for real, but keep a light touch, or it simply won't work. That's what's brilliant about this: there's a real sense of fun about it, but you still want to believe in it, too."

The humour isn't always so light, though...
"No, but even in the darkest situations things can seem quite funny. Writers like Ibsen and Chekhov have some very dark characters, but they also have this huge humour, and I think Torchwood has that quality, too. What runs through the whole script is wit, really, and I don't think drama can work without that."

Did you ever imagine you'd find yourself playing a part like this?
"I'm always amazed at what a rich career I've had, on telly and in the theatre. I've mostly been very lucky, though I had a bad fall a few years ago. That meant I didn't do much acting for a while, but now I've got new titanium knees, and I can spring about like a lamb. The drawback is when they set the alarms off in airports!"

Director Ashley Way watches procedings on a monitor, while the real action goes on behind.

Remembrance Of The Daleks

Boom Town

Something Borrowed

👁 SPOTTED!

If you think that you've seen Gwen's father, **William Thomas** somewhere before, he also appeared in the 2005 Doctor Who story Boom Town, and the classic series story Remembrance Of The Daleks, making him the only actor to have appeared in all three of those shows!

allowed to stay where it has been for over 200 years. The short-lived stunt window, meanwhile, was erected on a freestanding frame nearby.)

Not all the wedding guests are booked for the whole day, so after lunch Ashley has to decide where to position the remaining extras to achieve the shots he needs. In this afternoon's scene, the guests scatter in all directions, as Jack and Tosh crash the wedding and confront the Nostrovite.

Trying to direct this many people in organised chaos quickly becomes quite Pythonesque: "Do you want these two to stay in the room?" asks assistant director Paul Bennett. "No, he's not to leave the room, but she doesn't stay in the room with him..." replies Ashley, knowingly.

On rehearsal, the supporting artists get sufficiently animated that Ashley has to shout "cut!" three times before they stop running around. After that, it's time for a take, and the red carpet is quickly swept and hoovered, as Naoko Mori picks up her handbag and a gun that's not much smaller. John's revolver is jammed, so it gets a surgical seeing to with a hammer, and then everyone is ready to go.

A sequence of takes from various angles goes surprisingly smoothly, and when it comes to shooting from Jack's point of view, Naoko copes remarkably well, considering she is being bear-hugged by John, just out of shot.

"People don't realise the heartache we go through for something like this!" Ashley laughs, as the number of takes rack up. "For this episode, we've got five locations for the wedding alone. There's this place today for the ceremony and another for the exteriors, then three different hotels for the bedrooms, the corridors and the main entrance hallway.

"We can't go off schedule, or spend too long at one place, because they're all working venues. We only got this place because they're refurbishing the kitchens. Originally, we were going to build a bathroom in studio as well, but we moved the cocoon scene into the bedroom, which is probably more appropriate."

As the day winds down (around 6pm is a mercifully early finish by Torchwood standards), Ashley is philosophical about the work that goes into making a modern marriage.

"As with any episode, there were elements that we had to scale down," he says, "but we've still got a big Welsh wedding and Nerys Hughes running around with red eyes and big sharp teeth. At the end of the day, that's pretty much all you need, really, isn't it?" 🔲

Rhys

Gwen

Monster

By Joesph Lidster

Owen Harper is smiling down at me. I'm going to die.

My name is Paul Talbot and I'm twenty-seven years old. I was born in Cardiff and I work for an insurance company. I'm precisely six-feet tall and wear odd socks. My favourite television programme is Midsomer Murders but I tell people that it's The Wire. I've got strawberry blond (not ginger!) hair and I'm a Scorpio apparently. Oh, and I don't believe in God.

Well I didn't use to believe in God. Right now, lying on an autopsy table, I'm desperately hoping that there's a God or a Buddha or whatever, because right now I'm bloody terrified.

"I'm scared to close my eyes because I know I'll never open them again."

"Then keep them open," Owen says, still smiling. "Face death head on."

That's easy for him to say.

My eyes had opened that morning to a rush of light and pain. I was on the sofa. Still in my suit. My first thought had been to check I'd got everything. Patting down pockets. Wallet... Phone... Keys... Cigarettes... Everything in place, which was a relief, but then, as I sat up, the world spun violently around me and I ran to the loo and threw up. Then I staggered back to my feet and looked in the mirror. I stared at my reflection, feeling ashamed, and decided that I'd never again let myself be dragged out with the guys from work.

"You're twenty-seven," I told my reflection. "You really need to change."

Then, I closed my eyes and tried to remember where we'd been; who else had been there; what we'd drunk; how I'd got home — the usual Saturday morning questions. And then I realised I couldn't remember. It wasn't just a blur. It wasn't just, *Oh yeah, had a few pints and then... what, vodka?* I couldn't remember any of it. I sat down on the edge of the bath, a bit freaked, and thought back. Dave had gone round the office asking if anyone wanted to go to the pub. And I remembered that, obviously, I'd gone along. And I remembered that I did have a pint and then... I'd left! I had, I'd left the pub after one pint and I'd come home.

That was just the first in a series of improbable events.

So, I wondered as I staggered back through to the living room, *why do I feel like death?* I slumped down onto the sofa and just tried to remember. I was used to waking up confused, not knowing how I'd made it home, but this was different. This wasn't the drink. This wasn't a night out. This wasn't anything like that. I'd left the pub after one pint and I'd...

It had been getting dark but there'd been plenty of traffic. I remembered walking, listening to my mp3 player and getting irritated because one of the earpieces wouldn't stay in properly. There'd been a car waiting at the traffic lights. Inside, a couple arguing as they waited for me to cross. A light drizzle falling. Crossing the road as I listened to some old Nirvana track. So yeah, all a bit grim, but I'd left the pub after one pint. I was walking home sober. On a Friday night! So I was feeling good. And that's when something hit me.

I stood up from the sofa and might have actually put my hand over my mouth. You know, like they do on telly when they're in shock? Something had definitely hit me. Not a bloke or anyone. There'd been a sudden rush of light and then... bam! *Mebbe it was the chavs in the car?* But no, I remembered, they were still stuck at the traffic lights. It had been more like a shock. An electric shock.

Bam! A loud bang made me jump as my flatmate came bursting in through the front door. Chris was twenty-five and worked in computers. I think he designed websites or something, but it confused me so I never asked about it. I kind of regret that now. He was carrying a couple of carrier bags which he dropped onto the table.

"Man, it's roasting out there!" he said.

I noticed the damp patches under his arms. His forehead glistening. As he came closer, I could smell the sweat.

"You okay? Saw you passed out on the sofa."

"Erm... yeah," I muttered. "Yeah, I'm fine."

He started taking stuff out of the carriers. Eggs, bread, bacon, orange juice. I must have been staring at it...

"Yeah, all right, I'll do you some breakfast, but next time it's definitely your turn," he said, grinning.

His voice was starting to hurt my ears. I didn't know what it was but, yeah, it hurt. And I realised I was starving. Not just... well, you know when you're really hungover but all you can do is smoke for the first couple of hours and then you're suddenly so desperate for food? You'd eat anything because your body's going to just stop working if you don't eat right now? That's how I felt. Chris's voice was slicing through my mind and I could feel my heart beating faster and faster as I felt bile sloshing about in my stomach, desperate for food. Desperate to eat right now.

And that's when I realised that I wasn't looking at the food. I was looking at Chris. I was smelling his sweat, hearing blood pumping, his blood, my blood, and I was rushing towards him and the last thing I remember seeing is that half-smile he always did when he wasn't sure why something was funny. Like when we watched *Gavin and Stacey.*

When I opened my eyes again, I was confused. I was lying on the carpet and I could taste something in my mouth. It wasn't orange juice. I reached up and put my hand on the arm of the sofa, supporting myself as I staggered to my feet.

"Chris?" I called, confused. "I think I passed out... You there?"

There was no reply. I looked over at the table and saw the eggs, the bread, the bacon, the orange juice and what remained of Chris.

I screamed as I staggered backwards. Chris's blood was dripping onto the floor. Both from the table and from my mouth. I screamed and screamed as I stared at his body, what remained of it, and I knew, I knew instantly and unequivocally that I'd done it and the worst thing was that I didn't feel sick. Blood and sweat still moving slowly down my throat and settling the bile in my stomach. Chris tasted good.

After a while, I stopped screaming and collapsed, my back against the sofa, my eyes looking down at the carpet. Away from Chris. I tried to stop panicking. Breathed deeply. Wanted to grab a carrier and breathe into that but they were covered in hair and blood and guts and... I breathed deeply. Tried to calm myself. Tried to work out what had happened. Tried to be logical. What was I? I even laughed as I thought it... Was I a vampire? That was just stupid because vampires don't exist and, coughing up one of Chris's teeth, I realised I'd done more than drink his blood. Then, once I started laughing, I couldn't stop. This was me, Paul Talbot! I'd always been freaked as a kid if someone sucked their finger after they cut themselves. I'd always been terrified that if you did that and found yourself liking the taste of blood then would you want more? But now, come to think of it, blood tastes quite nice anyway... sort of warm, thick... like... like a thick meaty cup of tea. I kept on laughing, yeah, hysterical. I'd attacked and eaten most of my flatmate. Chris Manning, twenty-five, no longer working in computers. Then I stopped laughing and started crying. But I wasn't crying because of Chris. I wasn't crying because I'd killed someone. I wasn't crying because for some mad terrifying reason I'd killed my flatmate and eaten him.

I was crying because I was so so hungry.

Rushing out of the flat and down the stairs to the main exit, I stopped suddenly as I saw my reflection in the tinted windows in the hallway. If I had a reflection then, logically, that meant I wasn't a vampire. I think I might have felt, oh, about a nanosecond of comfort before the hunger made me retch and scream out. I ran out into the street. People were swarming about, enjoying the weekend. I could see them but it was the smell... oh, the smell! So much sweat and blood and perfume and deodorant. All the different people, the different smells, the different tastes...

I didn't know where to go or what to do. Hospital? And say what? That I was ill? Or maybe to the police, but then I'd get arrested and go to prison and I can't. It's not... I shrieked out again as the hunger ripped through my body, vaguely aware of people staring at me. A girl, must have been about seven years old, was suddenly looking up at me, asking me if I was okay. She looked so small it made me dizzy. I felt the hunger rising again but, terrified, I forced it back and screamed at her to go away. Well, actually I swore at her but that's not something I'm proud of.

I was running through the shoppers. I was on St Mary Street. I could hear sirens and talking and cars and laughter. All the noises battering me, hitting me, making me want to lash out and make it all stop and I was so hungry. You can't understand how hungry I was. And I ran down an alleyway, away from the crowds, away from everything. I worked out that logically I needed to go to my parents. They could help me. I'd tell them that there was something wrong and they could help me.

Protect me.

Save me.

My mum always helped when I was a kid and she'd help me now. She'd hug me. One of those big comforting hugs where all you can smell is... I screamed out again then collapsed against the wall of some old nightclub. Tried to get the thoughts out of my mind. Tried to stop thinking about the hunger and tried to remember who I was.

"You all right, mate?"

I looked up as a voice cut through the air. A woman. A waitress? It looked like she'd come out of the nightclub. She had... actually, I don't know what colour hair she had. Or how old she was. Or anything. Because as soon as I looked up, everything went black.

When I opened my eyes again, I gasped as the sunlight smashed into me. Everything seemed so bright. Even the woman's blood on my hands seemed to be glowing. I licked my fingers clean and staggered off down the alleyway.

'You're thinking about it, aren't you?' Owen asks.
I nod, trying not to blink back the tears. Afraid of the dark.
'You shouldn't,' he says. 'It's not healthy.'
I smile weakly as I continue working against the restraints.

I've no idea how long it took me to get to my parents' house. They lived all the way out in Grangetown but right then I felt like I could run forever. I was animal. Unable to think; unable to stop. Just needing food. The part of my mind that hoped Mum and Dad could help was gone. Mrs Monroe, the woman next door, saw me as I ran up the street and she started to ask me something, then must have noticed the blood down my clothes because her eyes went

wide. I punched her out of the way and, kicking down the door, barged into my parents' house.

"Mummy," I howled. That made me stop for a moment. Because I did. I actually howled. It wasn't my voice. As I ran through the hallway, I caught glimpses of my reflection in the array of family photos. But it wasn't my reflection. It was something else and I didn't stop to find out what. I ran through to the kitchen, knowing my mum would be there. It was like... it was like my mind was working in a different way so all these facts were there, you know? It was Saturday. About two in the afternoon. So my mum would have been shopping and would now be in the kitchen, making a late lunch for her and Dad. And it was sunny so they'd take it outside to their little back garden. All these facts that I'd never really realised I'd known... and I knew instantly why I was thinking about them now. I was thinking about my prey. It was tactical. I knew where they'd be so I could... I howled again as I kicked down the kitchen door.

And then I stopped. Mum and Dad weren't there. Five people were standing like soldiers, all pointing guns at me. For a second, I panicked. I'd never seen a gun before and, trust me, it's not nice seeing one pointed at you. I tilted my head and sort of whimpered as the group pointed their guns at me and one of them was shouting at me to stop.

"Stay where you are!" He was American. A big handsome man who didn't smell of sweat. He smelt of so much more. I examined him, trying to work out what he was. Was he a hunter or was he prey? He was powerful; I could taste that. I howled again and turned away from him. I looked at the others. Two women who smelt good and a man who smelt... of nothing.

"Why don't I want you?" I ask Owen.
"Because I'm dead," he replies.
I try to think about that. I try to think about what that actually means, but all I can do is remember what brought me here.

Too late, I remembered that there'd been five of them. There'd been three men but one of them was suddenly now behind me, and he was spraying something in my face! It choked me, made me vomit all over Mum's new kitchen floor. I lashed out at him, punching and scratching. I sent him flying into some cupboards which smashed open at the force. I was howling now, really howling. I lunged at the others, desperate to kill and eat and taste and stop the hunger, but then... the spray started to work. Everything started to go black again. The last thing I heard was one of the women...

"Jack... tell me we can save him..."

And everything went black.

When I opened my eyes that time, part of me was grateful not to see the remains of prey but part of me was instantly crying out in hunger. I wanted to hunt and eat and taste. I wanted the hunger to stop.

I was in... Well, God knows where I was. It was big. Really big. Stone and brick walls, metal gantries, computers and things I couldn't recognise and what looked like the water tower from Roald Dahl Plass holding the whole thing together. As I looked around, trying to take it all in, I was already realising that I was strapped into a chair. I was trapped and I couldn't feed. I started to howl as the pain in my stomach ripped through me.

"Can't you give him something, Owen?" asked the American. "I never liked a screamer."

I turned to look at the man, the one with no smell, coming towards me. He shrugged at me as he plunged a needle into my arm.

"What was that? What the hell are you putting in me?" I shouted.

Owen stepped back. "It's just an anaesthetic. Hopefully it'll stop you... hurting."

I started to cry with relief as I felt my body going numb. Losing the hunger.

Owen looked embarrassed and backed away. The American took his place, filling my vision. The stench of power was overwhelming.

"You've been causing us all sorts of trouble," he said. "Not only have you killed two people but you've hurt Ianto, and only I'm allowed to do that."

I glanced over his shoulder at the man I'd beaten up in my mum's kitchen. He blushed.

"I'm sorry," I muttered. Then I turned back to the American. "I've killed two people..."

He nodded. "And it's not even dinnertime."

I blinked. I remember looking at him and slowly blinking because I wasn't sure whether I'd heard right. I stared right into his cold eyes.

"You think this is funny?" I asked. "You're making jokes about it?"

He looked surprised. "You're the one killing people."

"Because there's something wrong with me! I can't stop!" I was screaming in his face now.

"Jack, let me talk to him." It was one of the women. She gently pushed the American, Jack, out of the way and crouched in front of me. She rested a hand on my arm. "My name's Gwen Cooper. You're Paul Talbot, right?"

I nodded.

"Okay, Paul, now nobody thinks this is funny. We want to help you but we need to know what's happened."

She was so close to me. I could smell her deodorant, her perfume and... underneath, fighting to escape, I could smell the real her. Just another animal. I could smell her blood and sweat... I could taste it on my tongue... I needed to...

"Get back!" I screamed.

She fell back just as I found my mouth lunging towards where her neck had been.

"I'm sorry! I'm sorry!" I cried out. "I can't stop it."

Jack folded his arms and looked over at Owen. "The anaesthetic?"

Owen shook his head. "Sorry, Jack. But I don't know what else I can do for him right now. We need to know what he is."

"He's human," called a voice. I looked up to see the other woman sitting at a set of computers. "I've got his birth certificate, his driving licence... which school he went to. He's Paul Talbot and he's human."

Jack moved over to her. "Thanks, Tosh. And you're sure he's not one of the sleeper agents?"

She shook her head. "No. He's human but he's changing."

"Jack, I can run some tests, try and work out what he's turning into." This was Owen.

Ianto came over and joined them, carrying a tray of coffees. "You sure, Owen? You really want to be alone with the Tintin monster?"

Owen turned and stared at him. "The what?" he asked, quietly.

Ianto pointed at my hair.

Owen looked like he wanted to sigh, then suddenly he started shouted at Ianto. "This isn't a bloody freak show!"

I stared shocked as Owen kept on shouting. He was ranting about gunshots and death and hunger. The woman Tosh was already at his side, holding him, trying to comfort him. Ianto was, like me, just staring, terrified at the doctor's rage. Jack and Gwen were pleading with Owen to stop. The noise was hurting me and I closed my eyes,

trying to block it out. I could hear myself howling as hot tears poured down my face. And then I realised it wasn't just the noise. It was the hunger, the endless sodding hunger. I was crying because I was starving. And everything went black.

"Why did you get so angry?" I ask Owen.

"Because," he replies, "I know what it's like when something happens to you. I know what it's like to be changed, to have your life taken away from you in an instant."

"And that's it?"

He shakes his head. "You've got everything I've lost."

I opened my eyes and lifted my head. Tosh was back at her computer. Gwen was sitting on a sofa next to Jack. I could see Ianto at the far wall, staying in the shadows.

"Where's Owen?" I asked.

Jack looked surprised that I'd even registered the man's name. "He needed some space. He's working on a cure for what's happened to you."

Gwen turned to face Jack. "In a way, it's probably healthy that Owen got so angry. He's not keeping it all locked away."

Over at the far wall, Ianto growled.

Tosh turned to look at me but stayed sitting at her desk. "I've been tracing your movements over the last couple of days. Did something happen to you last night?"

Trying to stay in control, I nodded. I could feel the hunger rising again but I knew these people wanted to help me. "There was a flash... I was walking home and... It was like lightening."

Tosh nodded then turned to look at Jack and Gwen. "That matches what I've found. Last night, Paul was walking down Barrett Street at the precise moment I registered some very minor Rift activity."

"You mean he was taken?" Gwen jumped to her feet. "Taken and then brought back?"

Tosh shook her head. "I don't think so. I think a tendril of Rift energy connected with him. It was so small, almost nothing, but it's changed him."

Suddenly, Owen was standing behind me. "And like Tosh, I've been running some tests. Paul's DNA... it's mutating. The Rift energy is in his body and it's changing what he is."

Jack stood up and moved to join Owen. Standing so close to me, I whimpered as I smelt his power. He smelt delicious.

"But I've been hit by Rift energy before. We all have to some degree. Why has it changed Paul?"

Owen and Jack looked over at Tosh but she shook her head. "I don't know. We only just found out the Rift can take people as well as bring stuff to us." She frowned. "Jack, we're aware of just the very basics of what the Rift can do. Paul was simply in the wrong place at the wrong time."

I had no idea what they were talking about. I didn't know what this Rift thing was. All I knew was that I was hungry. I needed to eat. I closed my eyes, trying again to block it all out, but then I heard Owen. His voice was quiet. Dark. Terrifying.

"And I can't save him."

Anger and hunger built up inside me. I could smell their sweat, their guilt, their pain. I could smell Tosh's pity, Gwen's sympathy, Ianto's fear. I could smell so much trapped down wherever we were. Death and things that weren't even human. Monsters and demons and lust and coffee. But over all this, Jack's power. It was overwhelming, suffocating me.

And I needed to eat.

I needed the hunger to stop.

I screamed with rage, my arms snapping through the restraints, and I lunged at Jack, my teeth biting into his neck, and I could taste so much...